W9-BAG-673

Jack W. Hayford
REBUILDING
THE
REAL YOU

God's Pathway
to Personal
Restoration

GL
Regal Books
A Division of GL Publications
Ventura, California, U.S.A.

Published by Regal Books
A Division of Gospel Light
Ventura, California, U.S.A.
Printed in U.S.A.

Regal Books is a ministry of Gospel Light, an evangelical Christian publisher
dedicated to serving the local church. We believe God's vision for Gospel
Light is to provide church leaders with biblical, user-friendly materials that will
help them evangelize, disciple and minister to children, youth and families.

It is our prayer that this Regal Book will help you discover biblical truth for
your own life and help you meet the needs of others. May God richly bless
you.

*For a free catalog of resources from Regal Books/Gospel Light please contact your
Christian supplier or call 1-800-4-GOSPEL.*

Library of Congress Cataloging-in-Publication Data

Hayford, Jack W.
    Rebuilding the real you.

        1. Christian life—1960-   . I. Title.
BV4501.2.H3688   1986   248.4   86-6646
ISBN 0-8307-1156-2

12 13 14 15 16 17 18 19 20 21 22 / 99 98 97 96 95 94

Rights for publishing this book in other languages are contracted by Gospel Literature International (GLINT). GLINT also provides technical help for the adap-
tation, translation, and publishing of Bible study resources and books in scores
of languages worldwide. For further information, contact GLINT, Post Office
Box 4060, Ontario, California, 91761-1003, U.S.A., or the publisher.

Contents

PART THREE   SUSTAINING THE CITADEL

Acknowledgments

My thanks to those the Lord used to ignite this book in me and release it through me: to Dan Vigna who prayed and to Ralph Mahoney of World MAP, Pat Robertson of the Christian Broadcasting Network and Paul Crouch of the Trinity Broadcasting Network. Further, with appreciation to Chuck Shoemake whose pastoral partnership over many years in helping people to wholeness has been both a teaching as well as a help to me.

I'm humbled by the tireless help of my secretaries, Janet Kemp and Sandy Turner, whose patience and persistence have been so supportive and encouraging.

Also, I wish to give special thanks for the assisting work of Susanne Mahdi, Carol Lacy and my mother, Dolores Hayford.

And finally to the team at Regal: Bill Greig for believing in the project and inviting me to do it; Fritz Ridenour for friendly understanding at points of delay; and Joan Bay Klope for helpfulness and graciousness as we pursued the final editorial process.

To these my gratitude: "The Lord gave the word: great was the company of those that published it" (Ps. 68:11, *KJV*).

Preface

"Can any good thing come out of Nehemiah?"

It seems appropriate to paraphrase the question raised by one prospective disciple of Jesus when he heard that Jesus was from Nazareth. Anyone from that God-forsaken caravan stop couldn't possibly rise to messianic possibilities!

Similarly, the book of Nehemiah—buried at the end of the Old Testament historical books—seems an unlikely prospect for contemporary, life-to-life relevance. If I had planned to teach a series on the ministry of the Holy Spirit to the individual believer, it would never have occurred to me to turn to Nehemiah.

One can almost hear the puzzled response. "Nehewhat?" Granted, I don't think I would have expected much from this short, crusty arrangement of historical events in and around 445 B.C. except for a peculiar confluence of two happenings.

First, Dan, one of our congregation's elders, stopped me after church one day. "Jack, I was thinking the other day about the number of people who are reborn but have such a great difficulty getting their lives together. I felt the Lord impress me that I was to encourage you to bring a series of messages on that subject—something about the repairing of the human personality."

I stared back, rather blankly, then replied, "Well, I'll sure keep open to it—try to keep sensitive, that is."

"That's good enough for me, Pastor," Dan replied. "I'll pray for the Lord to give you something."

Dan must have prayed, because I don't remember thinking much more about it.

But the second event took place three weeks later when my wife, Anna, and I were asked to minister in Illinois. While there we were provided with a picture-postcard setting for our accommodations during this midwinter conference. It was on a small hilltop in the country, surrounded by snow-bedecked trees alive with flitting squirrels. It was for all the world a scene from a Currier and Ives print; delightfully suited for a few days of rest. I decided to do some serious Bible reading.

Now, by "serious" I mean the rapid coverage of long passages of Scripture. It's so easy in one's daily devotions, and in the close study of briefer passages that so characterizes a pastor's scholarly efforts, to miss the grand panorama of whole segments of the Word. So it was there, comfortably ensconced before the fire in the coziness of that setting, that I spent hours at a time reading with reasonable speed through the twelve history books of the Old Testament.

I swept through exciting territory—the dynamics, the drama and the disasters of Israel's rise and fall as a kingdom. Then I came to Nehemiah.

I seriously pondered skipping it.

Of course I had studied the book during my formal training and had read it a few times in through-the-Bible pursuits. It was, to my understanding, simply the historical record of the efforts of one man to assist the Jews who had returned from Babylonian captivity in the rebuilding of the walls of the city of Jerusalem. I knew the content: I was aware that there were several chapters with nothing more than boring lists and historical reviews. I was about to go on to the next book when I was prompted to stop and reconsider.

As I did, I prayed, "Lord, I don't ever want to take any part of your Word carelessly. I'm going to read this brief book rather than skip by it, but I'm asking you a favor. As I read, would you show me something fresh in it? In Jesus' name, amen."

I meant the prayer, but my faith was not particularly active in terms of my feeling expectant as I began to read. So as I started I wasn't looking for something special, new, clever or insightful. What happened was simply the result of our loving Father's gift to me.

I had read about three chapters when suddenly a sense of holy surprise came over me. I paused, musing, "This wall-rebuilding process is very close to being a picture of the way God restores people." And immediately Dan's words flew back to mind, and I laughed to myself, "I'll bet he's been praying." I went ahead, finished Nehemiah and Esther—the remaining books of Old Testament history—and scratched notes in the margins as I read. And although I had become more deeply impressed with the possibilities of the subject as I did, I was thoroughly unprepared for what would eventually take place as a result of that reading and Dan's earlier remark.

In the intervening years the book of Nehemiah has become a kind of "Handbook on Personal Restoration" for millions of people who have studied it with me. It began with an extended series in the midweek services at my pastorate, The Church on the Way, in Van Nuys, California. The tapes of that series traveled widely and (at the choice of our staff, who provided these tapes to assist people recovering from deep distress resulting from their past) became a staple in our church's pastoral counseling ministry. Through the ministry of World MAP—a missions assistance agency—I was not only allowed to present the series at one of their great summer conferences, but their global tape ministry spread the teaching to leaders on every continent. Mail began to increase, attesting to the validity of these insights in Nehemiah: the Word of God was *working* in people's lives.

Finally, through the widespread ministry of the Christian Broadcasting Network, I was invited to do the series via a weekly telecast. The teaching literally reached out to unnumbered masses of people, and I seldom visit any part of the country but that someone remarks on God's grace at work in them through that series on Nehemiah—so unlikely a source yet *alive* because it is His eternal Word.

Later, the Trinity Broadcasting Network carried an even more expanded video edition to millions, and as I look back on that day of reading in a setting that looked more like a Christmas card than a study hall, I marvel at what God began. I cannot begin to enumerate the number of dear people who have expressed the life-transforming, Christ-glorifying dimensions of renewal and personal restoration they have experienced through the study to which I now invite you. I feel like a third person, looking in on a teaching session, watching the Holy Spirit take truth and apply it from His eternal Word into your situation. It's a privilege to be the delivery boy of this message. And as I do, the greatest fulfillment is in the prospect that the Holy Spirit's highest and greatest ministry will be realized in you: Jesus Christ, the Son of God, will be exalted as the Spirit makes His Person and His work real to you and in you by the Word of the Father.

Jack W. Hayford

The Church on the Way
Van Nuys, California

PART ONE

Perimeters
of
Possibilities

*Jerusalem's walls now dashed, destroyed and
smashed beyond belief,
Display the pain of wounded people, burned
and gashed by grief.*

*But comes a Helper, One who sees within
those shattered parts,
A citadel of strength and joy, rebuilt
from broken hearts He loves and treasures.*

—J.W.H.

CHAPTER ONE

Rebuilding
the
Real You

*The finished product of a self-made man is
usually an example of poor craftsmanship.*

—Anon

"For I know the plans I have for you, says the Lord. They are plans for good and not for evil, to give you a future and a hope." Jeremiah 29:11, *TLB*

THIS IS NOT a self-help book.

That probably won't discourage anyone, because we've all had our nightmare experiences with "doing it ourselves." Every family has horror stories with humorous punch lines; retelling the time they dug up the yard, tore out the wall, unplugged the sink, tried to replace the toilet, blew up the engine, over-pruned the apple tree or cut the cat's claws and were almost killed doing it.

But this is a book about help; or, better yet, about a helper. And the best part is that the help He has is for you.

I want to start with that because I am somewhat suspicious of a trend quite discernable today. The publishing arena sparkles with the plethora of snappy titles and spangled covers—books that promise wonders for the reader.

I suppose the reason I feel as suspicious as I do is because I have found in myself an unusual fascination with the explosion of books on personality improvement, physical exercise, financial pyramiding, beauty and grooming, leisure and play, sex and sexuality, and so on. They're all interesting and some are insightful and somewhat helpful, but—and I say it without cynicism—*all* are considerably misleading.

They usually mislead because they promise too much and provide too little.

Whether or not a book claims to be able to "change your life for the better forever," the title or table of contents—or maybe just the dynamism of the cover artist's graphic design—can compel a hope, if not a firm supposition. The buyer may suppose that to read it can hold the real possibility that the given handbook will make "a new me"; that is, in at least that part of his life addressed by the author. But that promise, whether stated or not, is too much.

And such books can't help but provide too little. The fundamental grounds for hope in all self-improvement books is Man—you, me, us, we. As a starting place we may not be all that bad, but we're not really good enough. When you start with Man it's all you're going to get, and even though the presumption survives that *Man has what it takes,* the evidence is in and the facts are, it isn't enough. Strangely, even in this experienced, enlightened time, the tide of humanism still rises. The proposition survives that somehow the predestined hour of evolution's goal is upon us: Just a little help, a little push, and we'll be *there* (wherever *there* is). But having arrived at the conclusion of *all* Man's self-help programs, the results require the classic Charley Brownism: "How come we keep losing when we're so sincere?"

There Has to Be Something More

But as I said, I'm really not a cynic. I'm not even opposed to the notion that some marvelously incredible possibilities *do* exist in Man.

It's entirely reasonable to me that if the image of God was originally stamped on the human being, something very substantial, mighty and glorious is still there, notwithstanding any damage that has been done in the meantime.

This book is about discovering *those* possibilities.

It's also about how to deal with the damage that's been done.

Rebuilding the Real You has to do with three things and they're obvious in the title:

1. Personal recovery and restructure
2. Reality as contrasted with imaginary
3. Your personality, your hopes and your future.

However, in dealing with those things I must, from the start, let you know from what viewpoint each of the three is approached. This book's foundational proposition is true: There is a genuine possibility of personal fulfillment by anyone, in spite of anything his/her past may have held. It is the following approach to each aspect of the theme that makes that proposition credible—and possible of being proven by you.

First, with reference to *rebuilding,* I'm inviting you to come to terms with anything in, about or around you that is broken. I'm offering hope and my stance is one alongside you.

We have *all* experienced something of brokenness: hearts, homes, health, finance, dreams, relationships. They are all as breakable as bones and they're equally curable, though harder to set. We may not all be basket cases, but it's certain we all need the Doctor.

Second, with reference to *the real.* I believe in the ultimate, the consummate, the conclusive, the absolute, the final, the genuine—the real.

I believe in God.

I believe He is larger than life and yet the Fountainhead of it all.

I believe He is the Father of love and yet has the right to speak with authority to His children.

I believe He has given us His Word and yet He still whispers to human hearts in private seasons of the soul.

And I believe He sent the Messiah and that He has proven the Messiah's miraculous capacity for meeting mankind's need by raising Him from the dead. Nothing could be more real than that, and in the context of the reality of the Messiah's resurrection, there is nothing impossible for your life or mine.

Which leads to *you*.

What I believe about *you* is based on the fact I have counseled thousands in intimate, private and personal sessions. I also speak to tens of thousands publicly every week. The primary thing I've learned about people—about *you*—is the phenomenal fact of our *uniqueness* and our *unity* as human beings.

We're obviously unique because there is not another you or me anywhere. But we're remarkably alike—a unifying factor which has taught me that it is neither presumptuous nor impersonal to speak through a book, to a crowd, over the radio, by a cassette or via the television.

And what I further believe about you is: (a) that you care; (b) that you hope and (c) that you believe.

You care or you wouldn't have read even this far.

You hope because we all do. Dreams are not rare; they fill all our hearts and occupy all our minds.

And I believe that you believe.

That is not a difficult proposition because I believe everyone has faith: "As God has dealt to each one a measure of faith."[1] I am not saying everyone's faith is either perfect, accurate or functional. But it is there.

It takes studied effort and a deep commitment to "not believe," for faith can rarely be crowded out of a human soul. Disaster may burn it, tragedy smash it, injury bruise it or arrogance denounce it. But faith, like seed buried under concrete, is difficult to keep down permanently.

However, *your* faith is probably *ready*. Your faith may be active, alive and vibrant, and like mine, yours may be nourished by the truth of God's Eternal Word and His risen Son.

In any case, whatever your readiness to believe in God's loving purpose being fulfilled in you, I invite you to read further.

Let me encourage you to welcome a new dimension of "help" into your life—the help I referred to at the beginning and which comes in the person of a helper. I intentionally avoided capitalizing the *h* then, but now let me introduce this Helper.

His first name is "Holy" and He's the Spirit of God, called the Holy Spirit. He is as truly and completely God as either the Father or the Son. He is deeply personal, all powerful and ever-present. And He wants to make Himself known in the details of your life.

That He is one of the Three-in-One, as the creed puts it, need not be a problem if such theological questions trouble you. He doesn't mind our human limitations, for the Holy Spirit—indeed, God in any aspect of His Person—is fully secure enough to be comfortable with our finite understanding. He isn't running a heavenly quiz to see how much we know, for in the last analysis our salvation and our destiny will not be resolved by how *much,* but by *who* we know.

His mission—and He's decided to accept it!—is to maximize your potential by helping you to truly "get it all together." I think your perspective on both of you—you and the Holy Spirit—will be broadened and deepened as you pursue these pages.

I've been encouraged by the response of literally tens of thousands of people to think you'll enjoy both the *way* we study and the *means* by which we do it. The way is in our examining a seldom read book—Nehemiah—one of the history books in the Bible. The means is a step-by-step uncovering of a beautifully encoded picture of the Holy Spirit's Person, style and ministry, as seen in the life and work of Nehemiah.

So, let's move into it.

I promise it will mean much to *the real you:*

- The *you* God had in mind from the beginning

- The *you* that along the way has been taunted, tainted and tangled by test and trauma

- The *you* the Helper is ready to bring to fulfillment and to your highest destiny.

Note
1. Romans 12:3

CHAPTER TWO

Finding Yourself in History

When you discover your Creator is the Lord of all human history, it's easier to believe He can overrule your past and beget a different future.

—J.W.H.

"Hanani one of my brethren came with men from Judah; and I asked them concerning the Jews who had escaped, who had survived the captivity, and concerning Jerusalem." Nehemiah 1:2

IT WAS THE VISIT of a party of concerned Jews that started it all.

The story begins to seethe with action as, without preamble, the book of Nehemiah begins, flowing out of one of the most tumultuous times in Israel's history. At once we are thrust into a flow of events which require review, for only in familiarizing ourselves with the story's setting can we start to see ourselves in its lessons.

Nehemiah begins by describing a conversation between himself and a relative who has just arrived from Jerusalem, having come to Susa (Shushan) the ancient capital of the Persian Empire. The mention of his inquiry "concerning the Jews who had escaped"[1] brings us to the necessary beginning point of our historical study:

> What Jews?
> What escape?

A Historical Sketch

To best begin, we need a five-minute historical sketch of that adventurous season in Hebrew history. It not only will give a context to our study, but it is an excitingly fascinating story, too! So, to enhance our perspective on the pathway to rebuilding human personalities, "take five." Step back with me to a century when the Spirit of God converged the activities of a half dozen kings, a spate of prophets and a displaced nation. In the midst of it, don't be surprised to find yourself there!

The year is 446 B.C., and a full 90 years have transpired since one of the grandest moments in Jewish memory. Just under a century ago more than 50,000 Jews were released by the edict of Cyrus, ruler of the Medo-Persians. Through the leadership of a remarkable man named Zerubbabel, they had returned to Jerusalem. To say "they" returned refers to the Jews as a people, for, in fact, very few of the contingent who returned had ever been there before. The returning exiles were actually the children and grandchildren of people who had been taken captive during the conquest and ultimate destruction of Jerusalem by the renowned Nebuchadnezzar—dreaded monarch of ancient Babylon. Consistent with the methods of conquerors in that era, he not only leveled and burned their capital city, but sought to totally break the spirit of the captives. He removed them from their homeland to a distant culture, hoping thereby to dissolve their identity as a people and smash their will as individuals.

Prior to this destruction and actual exiling of these Jews, Nebuchadnezzar had earlier gained dominion over Judea and its capital city, Jerusalem. He had installed puppet kings to govern the area, to keep it both accountable to and taxable by him. But due to recurrent resistance and political rebellion against his government, the decision was finally made to sack the city and exile any remaining prisoners to Babylon.

During that period of the puppet kings Jehoiakim and Zedekiah, Jeremiah the prophet warned of judgment to come because of the Jews' willful disregard to live as God commanded. Jeremiah had even predicted their captivity would cover a period of 70 years. He further prophesied that after this period of time, the exiled people would be released to return to Jerusalem to restore their Temple and their worship of God.[2]

And it happened just like that.

Great Prophesies Fulfilled

An amazing combination of international events weave together to fulfill great prophecies by Isaiah, Ezekiel, Zephaniah and Haggai, and the result was the release of all Jews who wished to return. Cyrus issues the edict according to Isaiah's prophecy, a forecast all the more phenomenal in that the prophet had even named the ruler who would release the exiles a century before the man was even born![3]

Ezekiel the prophet, who had lived with the people through their captive experience in the regions of Babylon, foretold their return and the reconstruction of their Temple.

Ezra, the history writing priest, reported not only the return and rebuilding of the Temple, but described the difficulties encountered in that project—obstacles that were overcome through the spiritual inspiration of the prophets Zechariah and Haggai.

In other words, here in this swirl of prophetic and historic activities, God is at work restoring His people, while nations and their kings unwittingly bow to the performance of His will. The balance of world power swung from Babylon to Persia, and with the fall of the majestic city at the hands of Darius, the fate of the exiled Jews went into the hands of those who had conquered their conquerors.

It would seem all the more complex and unlikely that their release should be realized. But deliverance came right on schedule. In the year 536 B.C.—*exactly 70 years* after the first contingent of exiles had been transferred to Babylon—Cyrus ordered their release.

Nehemiah's words, "the Jews who had escaped," refer to those who, by the emperor's decree, were allowed to return and to begin rebuilding their city and their nation. As a people, they would never be the same. The impact of the Babylonian captivity on the Jews had one positive result:

polytheism, the worship of *many* gods, was forever expelled from their minds. Henceforth, only the Lord Jehovah would be their God forevermore, and Moses' words would live in their minds, as they do in ours to the present: "Hear, O Israel: The LORD our God, the LORD is one!"[4]

Accordingly, upon return their first major undertaking was to rebuild the Temple in Jerusalem. They were a people for whom the pure worship of the one true God was a priority. Ezra, that small book just preceding Nehemiah, records this rebuilding.[5] It took 20 years from the inception of the project, but the Temple was rebuilt, completed and finally dedicated in the year 516 B.C.[6] The promise of the Lord had returned to a formerly desolated people, and their restored relationship with the living God was manifest in the rebuilt Temple to which they would gather for joyous worship.

The Jews' Embarrassment

But since then, two more generations have elapsed. It is now 90 years later; 90 years since they returned and 70 years since their completion of the Temple. Nehemiah's concern centers on the fact that the city is *still without walls*. The reproach reported to him is obvious in its explanation. Here is a people who have been able to reestablish their worship, but the evidence of a reestablished rulership—a respectable capital city rising above the ashes of its past destruction—is not forthcoming. With nearly a century behind them since the first arrivals, and with more than 70 years elapsed since the rebuilding of their Temple, there seems little reason for this embarrassing situation. How readily and how justly might surrounding nations and peoples mock them: "Some God, Jehovah! What power do you attribute to a God who has squatting worshipers, but who is unable to endow His people with the ability to restore their ruling city as well as their Temple of worship!"

Nehemiah Responds

This is what occasioned Nehemiah's deep grief and growing concern. A city with a Temple but no walls was a blight upon the name of its people and a reproach upon the name of their God. So Nehemiah set himself to prayer, weeping, mourning and fasting.

The character of this man, who is introduced to us as a consultant or cupbearer[7] to the Persian emperor Artaxerxes, is profoundly evidenced by his willingness to care as he does. His concern for the comfort and fulfillment of his people transcends his own security, prestige and convenience. We will find him interceding (chapter 1), risking his life (chapter 2), securing their safety (chapter 4), obligating himself in their interest (chapter 2), unselfishly giving of his own resources (chapter 5) and committing himself to the completion of a task that will remove their shame (chapter 6). And thus our five-minute historical sketch concludes. We have not only met Nehemiah, but we have been introduced to his historical setting. And as we begin to see the man—the historic figure Nehemiah—something of a picture of the Holy Spirit emerges. That is, if you've met *Him*! Have you?

Notes
1. Nehemiah 1:2
2. Jeremiah 25:11; 29:10
3. Isaiah 44:28, Ezra 1:1-4
4. Deuteronomy 6:4; Mark 12:29-30
5. Ezra 3-6
6. Ezra 6:15
7. Nehemiah 1:11

CHAPTER THREE

Meeting a Forever Friend

I've found a friend, O such a Friend,
He loved me e'er I knew Him.
He drew my heart with cords of love,
And thus He bound me to Him.

—James G. Small[1]

"The words of Nehemiah the son of Hachaliah. It came to pass in the month of Chislev, in the twentieth year, as I was in Shushan the citadel." Nehemiah 1:1-2

"All these things happened to them as examples—as object lessons to us—to warn us against doing the same things; they were written down so that we could read about them and learn from them in these last days as the world nears its end." 1 Corinthians 10:11, *TLB*

HAVE YOU MET the Holy Spirit?

Had I asked, "Have you ever 'bumped into' the Holy Spirit?" the answer for everyone would be yes, for whether you recognize it or not, He has at one time or in some way touched you. The Holy Spirit, the *third* Person of the Eternal Godhead—Father, Son and Holy Spirit—is somewhat of a mystery to most people. Referred to for centuries as the Holy *Ghost,* a dimension of unreality if not spookiness has surrounded His Person for so long that relatively few people know how to think about Him. Let's try.

To begin, the Holy Spirit is personal.

God is. He exists. He is not some abstract force or distant cosmic influence. He is personal, and the Holy Spirit is one expression of the threefold deity who created us, loves us, redeemed us and longs to bring us to full maturity in life and to the realization of His created purpose in each of us. (If the idea of the Trinity—that God is three persons in one person—boggles you, don't be surprised. It does everyone, even studied scholars and theologians. I suspect we *ought* to be prepared for the inevitable fact that if God is as great as God should be, we should expect the very richness of His essential being to transcend our order and our grasp of things!)

Jesus shed a great deal of light on the personality of the Holy Spirit when He taught us that: (a) He is like Jesus Himself in character, temperament and works;[2] (b) His mission is to help us personally understand more and more about Jesus[3] and (c) He has come to abide—to stay with us, somewhat of a heaven-given Forever Friend.[4] The most cursory reading of John's Gospel, chapters 14 to 16, establishes this. The Holy Spirit is sent by the Father, in the Name of the Son, to be with each one of us and to help us. There's nothing spooky about that.

The Holy Spirit Enters at New Birth

The first thing to happen when a person comes to God the Father, and willingly receives the gift of life which comes through Jesus, the Son of God, is that the Holy Spirit enters that person's life. Jesus described Him as a "Comforter"—One who will remain beside you to help, to counsel, to teach and to strengthen you. His entering is only a beginning though, and the sensible believer in the Lord Jesus will keep open to the Holy Spirit's increasing desire to expand the evidence of God's purposes in his life.

The *fullness* of the Holy Spirit, the *fruit* of the Holy Spirit, the *gifts* of the Holy Spirit and, most of all, the abundant, flowing *love* of the Holy Spirit, are all expressions of God's intent in giving us His Spirit. In other words, to simply realize that the Holy Spirit entered when I received Christ is to grasp a precious truth. But I need to see more—to want more. The practical development of God's work in my life requires that I give a growing place to the Holy Spirit's working within me. The Comforter has come and His mission is to help us onward as growing sons or daughters of the Most High God.

The test of the presence and the validity of the Holy Spirit's work in a believer's life is established in the Word of God. He makes people more thankful, more loving, more generous, more considerate, more understanding; in short, more like Jesus. And so, since our study will have a great deal to say about the Holy Spirit's work in our lives, let us understand from the beginning that the whole objective is not to *displace* Jesus with an emphasis on the Holy Spirit, but to *replace* our weakness and personal inadequacy with the Holy Spirit's enabling presence. In this way Jesus Christ will be seen more perfectly in each of us.

Even among people who have experienced the entry of the Holy Spirit into their lives—that is, people who have received God's love and forgiveness through Christ's death and resurrection—there seems to be wide variations in response to the Holy Spirit. Some hesitate in their readiness or their ability to allow the Holy Spirit an ever-increasing breadth of space to work in their lives. Such hesitation or apparent inability often seems related to a person's depth of difficulty with life prior to his/her conversion.

All of us are notorious for not asking God's help until our backs are against the wall. Somehow, we humankind are persuaded either that we can manage by ourselves or that to "bother" God for anything other than a crisis condition would somehow impinge upon His patience. This habit of waiting until our circumstances are drastic usually means that by the time we finally open our lives to Christ, considerable damage has been done. The net result is that whatever our past, however gifted our capacity at survival, virtually all of us badly need the Holy Spirit's restoring work in our lives. The beginning of that work is when He is welcomed. The advancement of that process is when He is permitted full reign.

If you have never opened up to the beginning of God's Spirit working deeply and powerfully in you, the path to that entrance is through one clearly marked door: Jesus Christ, God's Son. He said, "I am the door . . . I am the way . . . No one comes to the Father except through Me . . . . Nor is there salvation in any other, for there is no other name under heaven given among men by which we must be saved."[5] To open your life to Jesus Christ is to welcome the Holy Spirit into your life at the same time, for "no one can say that Jesus is Lord except by the Holy Spirit."[6] Simple heartfelt prayer can establish a turning from your own way unto His. And from this beginning life is waiting to unfold in the will of God and by the Spirit of God.

The Holy Spirit Directs Growth

Having begun life in Christ Jesus, we shortly confront a crucial question: Since the power by which I *began* this life was by the Holy Spirit, what shall be the power by which I *grow* in this life? The answer is rather obvious: The same Spirit! But equally obvious is the fact that most of us are slow to draw on His enablement.

Paul wrote to the Galatians, "Having begun in the [life-power of the] Spirit, are you now [by the energy of your own flesh] being made perfect?"[7] We all need the same reminder: New birth isn't the end of God's program for us. His Spirit has started something by His power which He wants to advance with our partnership.

Now all I have said is probably easy enough to acknowledge. Any honest believer is quick to say, "I need to grow" or "I want to grow." But the pathway to growth is usually cluttered with obstacles, and the obstacles are usually present or problem hangovers from our past—past lifestyle, past habits, past attitudes or past sinning.

> Forgiven we may be and forgiven we are.
> Reborn we may be and reborn we are.

But the factual evidence of our past so often remains a present reality. The fact of past sin is often seen in some of its remaining fruit. Of course you can be absolutely certain that God has forgiven it all: "There is therefore now no condemnation to those who are in Christ Jesus."[8] This is a bright truth of my new God-given inheritance! But of equal, truthful certainty is the continuing presence of many personal problems bequeathed to you from your past. Your salvation solves the problem of your relationship with God, but it doesn't always dissolve the problems in your life. It opens the doorway to solutions, but only by walking through that door and patiently pursuing that way will those problems finally be resolved.

This fact stands out so clearly in the book of Nehemiah. Here is the story of a people who had been given a new lease on life but who were repeatedly embarrassed by their inability to demonstrate *complete* evidence of renewal. Their rebirth was in their return, but their recovery as a people was incomplete; a fact underscored by their inability to restore their capital city. It was all so long in coming— indeed, appeared *never* to be going to happen. But into this setting, having heard of their distress while in a distant land, comes a man—a kinsman named Nehemiah. And it is here in Nehemiah, as the leader of that rebuilding process by which the walls of Jerusalem were restored from the rubble of past destruction, that I began to see a mighty picture of the Holy Spirit at work in human experience.

I began to see it when noting how Nehemiah had been sent by the king, just as the Holy Spirit has been sent to us by our King—the Lord Jesus.

I was impressed that Nehemiah's work was to lead. He didn't do the job by himself or *for* the people, but taught them how to move forward in the rebuilding project; much the same as the partnering way in which the Holy Spirit comes beside us to help.

And I was impressed by the authority that Nehemiah brought to a downtrodden people; authority that engendered confidence and that rose effectively against those adversaries of the rebuilding project.

Nehemiah began to appear as an ancient photograph of the Holy Spirit at work, and with that picture in mind, I probed further.

Nehemiah: The Consolation of God

As I thought further on the meaning of Nehemiah's name, I discovered in my Hebrew resources this definition: "Nehemiah—the consolation of God—derived from *nacham,* to breathe strongly, to pity, to console; and from *Yah,* the sacred name of the Lord." In short, Nehemiah means "the consoling breath or spirit of God." Further background study revealed his name was built from a verb root which conveys the idea of "pity which becomes active in the interest of another." In it all, Nehemiah was not only beginning to appear as a picture of the Holy Spirit, his name was virtually synonymous with His. The first whispers of a parallel study in the ministry of the Holy Spirit unfolding in this book had hardly prepared me for the amazing discovery I made in the meaning of Nehemiah's name! And it was on these grounds that I began to proceed more boldly, with deepening conviction.

Could it be that centuries before the coming of Jesus— long before the gift of the Holy Spirit—God had implanted in His own Word a coded message about the Holy Spirit's ministry of recovery? Could it be that forecast in this piece of Israel's history, just as other spiritual truths were prefigured Old Testament events, a message of salvation's fuller provisions was foreshadowed? Could it be that the historical person, Nehemiah, without realizing it himself, was living out a picture being filmed for all times? Are we viewing a photograph of God's Spirit assisting us in our weakness and the recovery of all those ruined parts of our lives which sin has disintegrated? Was it all happenstance? Coincidental?

I became convinced that the book of Nehemiah had at least a threefold message:

1. Facts of Israel's post-captive history

2. Principles for cooperation among God's people at work together

3. Lessons in the Holy Spirit's processes of recovery in our personalities.

It is my firm conviction that this third application of Nehemiah is clearly intended and not accidental. I believe it was and *is* something of God's intent for our use of this book.

For all of the rich truths it contains—of historic information, of practical verities concerning leadership, of worthwhile principles for Christian living—Nehemiah is also a handbook on the pathway to personal restoration. Here is a guidebook on how the Holy Spirit comes to assist us in rebuilding our brokenness, to strengthen our weaknesses, and to lead us past our ignorance and into victory beyond the habits of defeat.

We are more than people who need rebirth—we need rebuilding as well. The Holy Spirit, whose workings are released in our lives when we receive Jesus Christ the Lord, awaits those who will let Him partner with them in the rebuilding of every part of life that is less than a present praise to God. The poet penned it well:

The Comforter Has Come

O spread the tidings 'round,
wherever man is found,
Wherever human hearts and human woes
abound;
Let ev'ry Christian tongue proclaim the
joyful sound:
The Comforter has come!

The long, long night is past,
the morning breaks at last.
And hushed the dreadful wail and fury
of the blast,
As o'er the golden hills the day
advances fast!
The Comforter has come!

Lo, the great King of kings,
with healing in His wings,
To ev'ry captive soul a full
deliv'rance brings;
And thro' the vacant cells the song of
triumph rings;
The Comforter has come!

O boundless love divine!
How shall this tongue of mine
To wond'ring mortals tell the matchless grace
divine—
That I, a child of hell, should
in His image shine!
The Comforter has come![9]

Notes
1. By James G. Small. Public domain.
2. See John 14:17.
3. See John 16:14.
4. See John 14:16.
5. John 10:7,9; John 14:6; Acts 4:12
6. 1 Corinthians 12:3
7. Galatians 3:3
8. Romans 8:1
9. By William J. Kirkpatrick. Public domain.

CHAPTER FOUR

Getting Life Back Together

Unlike all the King's horses and
all the King's men
who were unable to put Humpty together again,
we have a King who has a better program—
and with much more than mere
horsepower.

—J.W.H.

"And they said to me, 'The survivors who are left from the captivity in the province are there in great distress and reproach. The wall of Jerusalem is also broken down, and its gates are burned with fire.'" Nehemiah 1:3

WHAT HAPPENED WHEN man 'fell'?", the Sunday School teacher asked the little boy.

"I don't know," he answered with a puzzled expression. "Did he bounce?"

Most people have a better idea than that of what is meant by the "fall of man," yet it is important to our study that we have an agreed viewpoint on this foundational event in human history.

The Fall summarizes in two words the fact that man was designed with a higher estate and an innately superior destiny than he now generally experiences or realizes. The entry of sin into the world drastically changed everything. Man, created perfectly "in the image of God,"[1] was designed for large purposes and deep fulfillment. His capacity for self-will (even for disobedience if he chose) was not an inherent flaw in his nature, but a necessary potential to his makeup if *free* will was to be available to him.

The opening chapters of Genesis set forth three essential truths:

1. Man was created in God's image and with unimaginably high destiny and purpose
2. Man was given responsible dominion over the earth—a rule to be expressed in everything from family relationships to the subjugation of earth and its resources through creative development
3. Man's authority and ability to successfully exercise that rule would find its fountainhead

in continued obedience to and worshipful
relationship with his Creator.

So from the original, creative order, two features are
intended for mankind. *Relationship* and *rulership* are fundamental to our created purpose; and both have been broken
by the Fall. Without recovery, His design for us and destiny
through us is marred. We are unable to truly live without
God, find fulfillment apart from Him or experience His purpose in us until the impact of the Fall is dealt with.

It is important that we each have a sense of man's purpose and the dimensions of loss in his fall, for unless we
perceive something of what has been lost, we won't know
what we might expect to be regained through the full salvation Christ has purchased.

The Beginning of God's Redemptive Purpose

For the most part, Christian preaching and teaching
focus only on restoring people to a relationship with God;
showing how the cross of Jesus Christ has bridged the
chasm sin caused between God and man, and how salvation
offers man a way back to God. Of course this message is
absolutely necessary and is fundamental as a starting point
of understanding. We *must* be born again![2]

But if we stop there, with the acknowledgment of our
need for a restored relationship, we may fail to perceive
God's full redemptive purpose for fallen man. The restored
relationship is primary in sequence, but does not conclude
God's purpose in life for us. His desire is our return to
restored *rulership*. This means a recovery of self-control, of
personal identity, of stabilized temperament and character.
It means the fulfillment of Romans 5:17, that "those who

receive abundance of grace and of the gift of righteousness will *reign in life* through the One, Jesus Christ."

And it is reigning now in life—God's second follow-through goal in His redemptive purpose—that is at the heart of our studying Nehemiah's assistance to the citizens dwelling amid the rubble that was Jerusalem. The essence of the project does not focus on a restored relationship so much as it does a restored rule—the recovery of a godly people's identity as self-governing, and their city's restored appearance as a capital center of righteousness.

The opening conversation between Nehemiah and Hanani, a relative who visited him with a report from the returned exiles in Jerusalem, reveals the crux of concern:

"How is it going with our brethren who have returned to Judah?" Nehemiah asked.

"Those who have returned are in great distress and reproach," Hanani replied.

"What is the cause of their problem?" Nehemiah probed further.

"The wall of Jerusalem is broken down and its gates are burned," revealed Hanani.

Hanani's complaint focused on the embarrassment of a people who had solid evidence of a relationship with God. First, He had fulfilled His Word and returned the Jews to their land. Second, He had helped them in the project of rebuilding the Temple. Third, they regularly conducted faithful, God-honoring worship at the Temple site. In other words, their relationship was restored and their worship was pure.

But notwithstanding the joy of that right relationship with God, the people recognized the incompleteness of their situation: "We have a Temple, but our capital city—our center of government—is a shambles." You see, without a wall the city was open prey to oppressors. With destroyed gates there was no way of keeping back an adversary and no focus of government, for in ancient times the city gates were the seat of local rule. In short, they had a life with God but had no evidence of it affecting life's daily details. They were embarrassed. After all, this was their representative city—their "face" to the world around. But even though their Temple had been rebuilt, the rest of the city and the walls surrounding it were nothing but rubble. How vulnerable they were to the mockery of their critics and enemies: "Some God you worship in that Temple! Look at the mess you call your capital city. Apparently your God has little concern for or no ability in the practical matters of life!"

Have you ever sensed this dilemma yourself? Are you born again, yet parts of your personality are a contradiction to the power of the God you worship? Might someone justly point a finger and challenge, "Big deal! Some new birth. Look at the mess . . . !"? After taking note of details in your life and knowing how true it is that so much is broken down and burned with fire, you may feel that same sense of reproach and distress Hanani expressed to Nehemiah. If at any point you feel vulnerable to just criticism of practical weaknesses in the structure of your life for Christ, take hope. Nehemiah gives us a message about people who had a relationship with God, but moved on in that relationship to recover their potential to function during life's challenges, problems and practical details. That's what it means to "reign in life," as the Bible says. Or as contemporary jargon puts it, "to get it together."

So here in Nehemiah is a handbook on recovering what's been lost by sin. Here is the hope that our restored *relationship* with God can be matched by a restoration of rulership (a) by regained self-control (gates), and (b) by a reconstruction of the shattered dimensions of our self-understanding and purpose (walls).

The Rubble of the Past

Look at Israel in its past sin. As a nation, they had walked in disobedience, and because they had failed God, judgment came upon them.

Lest you misunderstand, be assured that such judgment is not so much an act of God's anger as it is simply the certain result of disobedience. Father God is injured and grieved, when through rebellion or ignorance we pursue our own way unto our own destruction. Yet His judgment is never vindictive. God does not even have to activate every instance of judgment upon sin. Most sinning bears in itself the deadly seeds of its own penalty. When the sin is sown, the judgment is as sure as harvesttime. People introduce judgment upon their own heads, and the destruction distilling from their failure so often leaves a sad residue—even after they have been saved.

And so it was that even though Israel had returned, had built their Temple, and as a people praised their God, the surrounding rubble was still sad and embarrassing evidence remaining from their past sinning.

And so often the same is true of us. How many are the ways in which we, the reborn, are a paradox—possessors of eternal life but dispossessed of a sense of solid personhood?

Have you ever asked,

"Why can't I shut depressive thoughts out of my mind?"
"Why am I so shaken by fears?"

"What causes my inability to defend against temptation? I feel like it's threatening to overcome me."

"Why do feelings of worthlessness prevail?"

Shouldn't our restored relationship with God be enough to keep out unwanted thoughts and demeaning attitudes? Or is there another aspect of our salvation available and waiting to be appropriated? Can the Lord reinstate His *rule* in me just as He has reinstated my relationship with Him? The answer: Absolutely!

And the starting place is to see *both* (a) the need and goal of such recovery and (b) the fact that the time it takes for our recovery process may differ from others.

Patience with Progress

Many believers have such a struggle trying to learn to walk as steadfast disciples of Christ while still so very crippled from their past. Although in sincerity they seek to speed ahead, before long they become frustrated and confused, especially when they see others who are progressing steadily.

But to become a new creature in Christ is only the beginning of this new life. The promise, "If any man be in Christ, he is a new creature,"[3] does not instantly guarantee completed products. It does promise a new world of possibility opening to us; we are no longer dominated or controlled by our past. But for the full dominion of Christ's rule to penetrate the whole personality, in most cases "the real you" needs to be rebuilt.

Consider the testimony of two radically different reborn babes in Christ under my own pastoral charge.

Thelma stepped into my office one Saturday afternoon in tears, having just been kicked out of their apartment by her husband. He was a satanist and they had both been heavily involved in the occult before her conversion to Christ. Her past involved a great deal of rejection by her parents and personal violation by her father. Though she was highly intelligent, and a product of one of America's finest universities, Thelma was virtually incoherent as she stood before me in tears. Here she was, bereft of support and the mother of two lovable little children who themselves were terribly confused by what was happening with Momma and Daddy. This combination of factors shaping her present was a staggering load for a young Christian. She unquestionably was Christ's—she was reborn! But the remnants of her past now converged to reduce her to an emotional basket case, a domestic wreck and a desperate spiritual dependent. Though she was a new creature in Christ, Thelma was a highly vulnerable babe who could hardly walk and was completely ignorant of what to do and how to do it. "Broken walls and burned gates" would aptly describe her.

For the following five years I watched her grow through the Word, through a fellowship with the body of the congregation, and by the assistance of wise counselors on the pastoral staff. The rebuilding process was long, but she eventually became an adequate, recovered person. Having long since been forsaken by her husband, God later provided a godly young man as His gift, completing the redemption of her domestic past.[4] I was witness to that marriage and delight to tell you that in every way Thelma is restored and her children are lovely, stable, happy kids. She has become what her name implies—an expression of "the will of God."

The second person is the kind of convert pastors wish could happen every time. It was a joy watching Edward respond as he went from new birth to stable discipleship within several weeks of his conversion. Within months he was given some leadership roles and within three years moved into eldership. He was recognized within the congregation as a growing-to-strength servant of Jesus Christ.

But Edward's former "walls" were considerably different from Thelma's.

His family background was solid and secure, having parents who lovingly raised him. He never knew the pain of parental rejection, for most of his life was spent experiencing every cultural, financial, educational, intellectual and emotional benefit a young man can receive. Moreover, he was raised in the context of a Christianized environment, in a church that reverenced God. Even though the Word of God and our universal need of new life in Christ was untaught there, the social influence was redemptive and moral values honored. Thus, though Ed had never heard a salvation message, he did have some knowledge of the Bible and a genuine desire for spiritual reality. He was successful in business, emotionally stable and economically and professionally secure. The simple fact is that Edward had little from which to recover.

He needed rebirth—everyone does. And he accepted discipleship—we all should. But Edward became firm in personal and spiritual stability much more rapidly than Thelma, although today their relative strength in Christ is virtually equal.

The whole point of these two illustrations is to dramatize the truth that some who have been Christians for *years* have Thelma-like problems from the past. Perhaps people are not as drastic in their circumstance as she was, but they still wish they knew how to get from where they are to where they want to be as Jesus' disciples. Sheer grit and determination is honorable while it lasts. But beside the fact that weariness usually takes over with time, grit and determination aren't God's way. Such so-called discipleship is nothing more than works built on grace, and given time, the temporary walls of self-worked righteousness will crumble. Most of us are among the vast number and variety of "Thelmas." "Edwards" are joyful and welcome exceptions, but very few people today have Edward's privileged background. Most of us are in considerable need of repair at the personal level (and even Edward would acknowledge points of rebuilding his own life required).

Since it is unlikely that I will experience the fullest sense of Christ's Kingdom rule in all my life until wholeness in my personality is realized, I need to let patience perform its perfect work. Some issues can be changed overnight through simple obedience to God's Word. But other problems of personal weakness, residue from the impact of past sinning, require time. Rebuilding alone will accomplish what rebirth makes possible, but does not instantly achieve.

The rebuilding stage of the Christian life is normal and its pathway clear: First, identify your "broken walls and burned gates." Second, partner with "Nehemiah."

This prompts two questions:

1. Can you identify where your personality has been eroded, broken, weakened or destroyed through marring experiences or sinful failure?

2. To deal with this, are you ready to receive the

Holy Spirit as your helper, enabling your
recovery of those points of pain or weakness?

He is able to make possible the transference of God's Word
into actual, practical, healing and restoring power in you.

Looking into this striking, historic picture, it is valuable
to also remember that those broken, burned walls—so
emblematic of our own personalities—were not always the
direct result of the people's own sin. Many inherited a condition not actually due to their own actions, for the city's
destruction was the price of another generation's failure.
Similarly, today many Christians are prevented or
obstructed from their "reign in life" through inherited difficulties or personality weaknesses "transmitted" to them
from an earlier generation. At times the transmission has
been through actions. Misunderstanding or mistreatment,
ministered unwittingly or intentionally by parents or other
authority figures, often stamps people with lifelong scars—
unless recovery occurs. Childhood innocence is often
tainted by adult ignorance and without redemptive action,
permanent emotional disability is experienced. Other trans-
missions are "genetic"—and genetics are not only physical
in their source: spiritual, emotional and mental residues
from varied influences are often discernable.

Of course, these observations are no attempt to white-
wash the fact that we have all contributed to a large share of
our problems. But it is appropriate to note (a) areas of need
and (b) that all answers to our own Fall are not instantly
provided through rebirth.

Nor is rebuilding always readily available by sincere
dedication to disciplines or through renouncing bad habits.

What we all need—each in distinct ways—is a rebuilding of ourselves; the setting in motion of a process to

recover our personalities until we operate like the city of the great King—a worthy capital for Christ as He exercises rule in all our personalities.

So where do we begin?

Notes
1. Genesis 1:27
2. John 3:3
3. 2 Corinthians 5:17, *KJV*
4. See 1 Corinthians 7:15.

CHAPTER FIVE

Recognizing Your Makeup

*Son, how did you put the jigsaw map of
the world together so quickly?
Because, Daddy, on the other side was
the picture of a man, and when
I put the man together, it
put the whole world together.*

—J.W.H.

"And they said to me, 'The survivors who are left from the captivity in the province are there in great distress and reproach. The wall of Jerusalem is also broken down, and its gates are burned with fire.' So it was, when I heard these words, that I sat down and wept, and mourned for many days; I was fasting and praying before the God of heaven." Nehemiah 1:3-4

WE'VE ALL DABBLED with jigsaw puzzles enough to experience the irritation of discovering missing pieces which disallowed our finishing and enjoying the picture. And I've watched the frustration of people who want to "see the whole picture" of God's purpose in their lives, but who don't understand how the pieces of their personality fit together. A surprising number of intelligent spiritual people have no real definition of the makeup of their personality or the constituent parts of their being.

Unnecessary bewilderment begins because most Christians do not know the difference between their soul and their spirit. Far more than an academic issue, the distinction between soul and spirit is just as clear as the difference between the broken walls of the city of Jerusalem and the Temple built within the city. Can you imagine the people supposing the completed, rebuilt Temple rendered the rebuilding of the walls unnecessary?

It is just as important for us to know this distinction of soul and spirit to best respond to God's work in our personalities. Since the Holy Spirit wants to rebuild all brokenness of soul, it will help to know exactly what goes on there.

Discerning Between Spirit, Soul and Body

The Bible makes a clear distinction between our soul and our spirit:

1. Hebrews 4:12 states: "For the word of God is living and powerful, and sharper than any two-edged sword, piercing even to the divi-

    sion of *soul* and *spirit,* and of joints and mar-
row, and is a discerner of the thoughts and
intents of the heart."

2. In Luke 1:46-47 after Elizabeth has greeted
her and confirmed her having conceived the
Messiah, Mary sang, "My *soul* magnifies the
Lord, and my *spirit* has rejoiced in God my
Savior."

3. In 1 Thessalonians 5:23 Paul prayed for the
Thessalonians: "Now may the God of peace
Himself sanctify you completely; and may
your whole *spirit, soul,* and *body* be pre-
served blameless at the coming of our Lord
Jesus Christ."[1]

The Bible not only distinguishes between man's spirit
and soul, but says that the Word *discerns* between them[2]—
that is, it teaches the difference to avoid confusion about
them. God's Word doesn't present the fact that we have
three parts to our being for reasons of philosophical argument. Neither is the tripartite nature some hangover of
ancient thought to be replaced today by newer notions. No,
God reveals the structure of our being by His Word, and
since He wants to accomplish distinct things in each part of
us, He wants us to understand about each part—from His
Word.

The geographic setting in the text of our Nehemiah
study provides an interesting and helpful parallel to the
structure of our own beings (see Appendix A).

First, consider the Temple: Central to the city and central to worship, it can be likened to the inner man—*the
human spirit.* Sin destroys our relationship with God and
our capacity to worship Him. Rebirth in Christ—like a

reconstructed Temple—makes renewed worship and fellowship with God a living possibility "in spirit and truth."[3]

Second, consider the city: Central to the rule of the surrounding land or territory, it can be likened to the center of individual choice—*the human soul.* Just as the walls and gates had been ruined by sin's judgment, so the impact of sin in the personality deteriorates the human capacity to will to live under God's will and rule—to "reign in life" through Jesus Christ.

Third, consider the environs: This area is intended to be a land of peace and fruitful harvest and can be likened to the *human body.* Through it, God may channel and manifest His Kingdom witness or it might manifest actions which contradict or violate God's purposes.

The Focus Is on the Soul

Nehemiah's dismay was specifically directed toward the fact that the walls of the city remained broken down long after the Temple was restored. The above parallel holds true here. The focus of concern on the walls relates to the need for our focus on our *souls.* There is an Old Testament picture of a New Testament truth in Nehemiah's words, "So it was, when I heard these words [Hanani's report], that I sat down and wept."[4] Hear the echo of the Holy Spirit's present concern over the activities of some reborn yet still "broken" souls. This is expressed in Paul's call to "Grieve not the holy Spirit."[5] His plea directly follows an appeal to recently reborn Gentiles to leave their former patterns of living behind.[6] Although he has addressed them as "saints"[7] (spiritually alive in Christ), they sometimes still fall into past practices.

See the parallel? Even though their *spirit* had been reborn (restored Temple), Paul calls to them to no longer walk (a) with a "darkened understanding"—with a *worldly mind* or (b) as those who live "past feeling"—led by *worldly emotions*.[8] He is dealing with "soulish" behavior, since the "understanding" (intellect) and "feelings" (emotion) are operational there, in the soul.

That Nehemiah's tears and the Holy Spirit's grief both center on the unfinished residue of brokenness (the walls and gates, which compare with the soul—intellect and emotions) helps us focus on that part of our being where the rebuilding process is most needed. It is more than coincidental that it is the *walls* which caused Nehemiah's tears and our *souls* which can cause the Holy Spirit to grieve.

Gaining this beginning insight, we can see ourselves as human beings—spirit, soul and body. When our spirits are reborn our bodies are subject to our direction. Now the soul, like a middleman who determines what of our new *life* will be translated into new *living,* sits in the driver's seat. If it is in anyway disfunctional by reason of past habit, pain or needed repair, the whole person is affected. Just as broken walls hindered the definition and control of the city, so the saved but unrestored human soul can hinder progress.

As the seat of our identity and will, the soul functions as the command center of the human being. What goes on there determines the extent to which the King's rule will be manifest in the whole of our being. If there is brokenness or malfunction there, it may not mean my damnation, but it does cause the Holy Spirit consternation. Let's further examine the way the soul works.

Your soul includes three essential facets and functions which essentially comprise your personality:

1. Your *intellect*—the processes of your intelligence, your mind, your thoughts

2. Your *emotions*—the processes of your temperament, your feelings, your attitudes
3. Your *will*—the processes of your choice, your determination, your decisions.

Most of what lures, drives, attracts, convinces, persuades or motivates you is generated at the *thought* (intellect) or *feeling* (emotions) level. Affected by this interplay of intellect and emotion is your *will,* the decision-making center of your soul.

The human will is the most awesome feature of the soul—indeed, of your whole being—for it determines destiny. By reason of the will, the soul functions as the command center of the whole personality.

What goes on in my soul determines how I *feel* today (my emotions).

What goes on in my soul decides if I will *learn* today (my intellect).

Those lessons I must *know* to grow in the understanding of the Lord. Those feelings I need to *respond to* or *reject* to obey the will of God. Those attitudes or facts I need to *process* according to the Holy Spirit's directives. All of this is going on *today* in my soul. How my *mind* and *emotions* interactionally function will generate *decisions* which either deepen my problems or release my progress. And with this understanding, the absolute need of my *soul* being restored becomes clearer than ever. My reborn spirit may make possible my worship of God, but my rebuilt soul is what will determine my service for Him.

All of us want the Lord to be glorified in *all* our thoughts and *all* our feelings, so that *all* our *choices* advance us in His way and in His will. Thus the reconditioning of our souls becomes a project of highest priority.

Action Ahead

In Nehemiah's concerned tears you can see a prophetic picture of the Holy Spirit's compassionate grief over any need you have and the fruit of this concern is that he will *act*. In the same way you can count on the Holy Spirit. He is moved with an understanding of your need and ready to bring aid to the site of any weakness in your soul.

His action will address specific areas of brokenness. All of us share much in common. Emotionally, much is residue from childhood experiences, from recent suffering, from disappointments leaving scars—often even when the scarring event itself seems to have been forgotten. And to emotional wounds of the soul are added those in the mind; a habit here, an insensitiveness there, a loss of capacity to respond.

Often what happened to you in early years breeds insecurity. Like a broken wall, no established boundary of identity or secured line of defense exists. In the same way "broken walls" hinder the capacity of the mind to resist unwanted ideas and cripple strength of emotion to be courageous or stable in crises.

Question: Why don't I seem to be able to resist temptation?

Answer: Could the basic reason be that crumbled walls and burned gates—burned with the hellfire of a past lifestyle—mean there is no line of defense?

Question: Why am I so easily overcome by doubt or by habit?

Answer: Could it be that the personality is spongy because the solidity of fixed walls is absent?

Further, by reason of the soul's pain, much physical agony may be latent or present. Physicians and psychologists attest that physical sickness is often the direct result of mental or emotional upheaval. Our souls (psyche) impact our bodies (soma) and our physical afflictions are often psychosomatic—signs of deeper pain within our personality.

How crucial a center the soul!

How needful its rebuilding unto wholeness!

How About You?

Are there some things going on in your mind that hinder your spiritual growth? Do you feel like those people in the book of Nehemiah—a reproach and an embarrassment to yourself so that you feel weakened or crippled in the face of your enemies?

At the mental level, do doubts become a real difficulty? How often does your imagination hinder you to the point that it interferes with where you really want to go? How about impure thoughts? How about the inability to focus? Do your thoughts digress to the unimportant and insignificant? How many times do your reasoning capabilities argue against you rather than work for you? How many times do things going on in your mind torment you and you find yourself incapable of withstanding them? I'm not talking about a lack in intellect; the issue has nothing to do with your I.Q. I am addressing the rubble—the things that don't seem to cooperate with what God is wanting to do and the part that cries out to have the mind of Christ.

And how about the "emotional you"? Do fears surround you? Do lusts clamor for attention, eroding your inner integrity and trying to prompt decisions to feed them? Does anger fester, embittering your attitude toward others? Has unforgiveness lodged deep within, hindering the kind of spiritual growth you'd like to have?

Oh, how these mental and emotional forces work against our *will*! They cripple our confidence, hinder our attempts to move ahead and weaken our resistance. And it all has to do with a soul needing restoration at points of loss.

Yet, amid all this and deeper still, dear friend, let a core of God-established hope abide: He has secured the Temple within! Your reborn spirit is alive toward Him! That life within guarantees the presence of the heavenly.

Nehemiah! The Holy Spirit Is Present to Help!

Your spirit (the *new* you deep inside) loves God unashamedly and unabashedly and you are owned—totally possessed by Him. You *are* saved and you *know* it. You have that deep settled confidence—I am the Lord's. In the past you might have looked at yourself and said, "If I am the Lord's, why am I like this?" But the answer is now coming into view. You are learning how God's restoration program is included in His gift of redemption in Christ. He *regenerated* you; He will *restore* you. Redemption includes a reborn spirit *and* a restored soul—a certain recovery of *all* that's been stolen in the past.

So, let's summarize.

Your soul is constituted of (a) your intellect—how you think; (b) your emotions—how you feel and (c) your will—the choices you make. All three are addressed in Paul's prayer: "May your whole spirit, soul and body be preserved blameless at the coming of our Lord Jesus Christ."[9] And the Holy Spirit is still answering that prayer today. So join your prayer to that one, and may this picture of your human personality give rise to your deeper heart cry: "Oh, God, according to your promise, I welcome your Holy Spirit to teach, to strengthen, to console and to restore me. Work your wholeness in my whole personality and make me like Jesus!" Amen!

Notes
1. From this reference onwards, all italicized words and phrases in Scripture quotations are added by the author for emphasis and clarification.
2. Hebrews 4:12
3. John 4:24
4. Nehemiah 1:4
5. Ephesians 4:30, *KJV*
6. Ephesians 4:17-32
7. Ephesians 1:1
8. Ephesians 4:17-19
9. 1 Thessalonians 5:23

CHAPTER SIX

Prayer
That Rebuilds
People

*I was praying in the Spirit one day,
and my Adversary whispered, "That doesn't
sound like much of a prayer to me."
And I answered, "And that, you scoundrel, is
because I'm not talking to you."*

—*J.W.H.*

"So it was, when I heard these words, that I sat down and wept, and mourned for many days; I was fasting and praying before the God of heaven. And I said: 'I pray, LORD God of heaven, O great and awesome God, You who keep Your covenant and mercy with those who love You and observe Your commandments, please let Your ear be attentive and Your eyes open, that You may hear the prayer of Your servant which I pray before You now, day and night, for the children of Israel Your servants, and confess the sins of the children of Israel which we have sinned against You. Both my father's house and I have sinned. We have acted very corruptly against You, and have not kept the commandments, the statutes, nor the ordinances which You commanded Your servant Moses. Remember, I pray, the word that You commanded Your servant Moses, saying, 'If you are unfaithful, I will scatter you among the nations, but if you return to Me, and keep My commandments and do them, though some of you were cast out to the farthest part of the heavens, yet I will gather them from there, and bring them to the place which I have chosen as a dwelling for My name.' Now these are Your servants and Your people, whom You have redeemed by Your great power, and by Your strong hand. O Lord, I pray, please let Your ear be attentive to the prayer of Your servant, and to the prayer of Your servants who desire to fear Your name; and let Your servant prosper this day, I pray, and grant him mercy in the sight of this man.' For I was the king's cupbearer." Nehemiah 1:4-11

JOSH BILLINGS, the American humorist, is credited with saying, "Never work before you eat your breakfast; but if you ever *do* have to work before you eat your breakfast, eat your breakfast first."

Let me play off Billings's counsel and relate it to undertaking the restoration of the human personality: "Never attempt a spiritual activity before you pray; but if the circumstance demands activity before you pray, pray first."

One thing should be apparent from start to finish: Nehemiah believed in the power of prayer and seeing the results he received, we should, too.

There are no less than 17 prayers in the 13 chapters of Nehemiah. This first prayer demonstrates some basic truths we all need concerning the possibilities of prayer and recognizing its power base.

The prayer Nehemiah made sets the exact tone, truth and thrust of the kind of praying the Holy Spirit assists believers in making. The starting point, however, is in *committing* to pray. The will to pray is often weak and this is due to more than just our fleshly procrastination. So many people are uncertain as to the real possibilities of prayer:

> What can I pray for or about?
> When should I pray?
> How can I pray *in* God's will (I don't want to be presumptuous!)?
> How can I be sure I'm not praying selfishly?

And worst, because this attitude is blindest of all:

Maybe things will work out anyway.

Such uncertainty breeds passivity toward prayer. In reading this prayer of Nehemiah's—a model of its kind— we can learn much, for it resulted in a restored city. Your praying the way Nehemiah did can result in restoration too! So come, seriously willing to let God's Word instruct you.

The record of Nehemiah's prayer shows some basic pointers to the pathway of prayer.

Prayer Isn't "Earning Points"

Before we actually analyze the principles of prayer demonstrated here, let us be sure we understand what is and is not a correct approach in prayer. Contrary to many people's ideas, prayer is not another kind of work. While there is a ministry of prayer, it is not a means by which you earn points with God or a fleshly attempt to gain God's attention or favor through your human effort. Getting God to restore His image in you is not a reward He gives in response to a certain quantity of prayer. God is not looking down condescendingly, watching to see when you have bowed and scraped enough to receive a holy fortune cookie, an ego-stroking pat on the head or a paternal smile. Prayer is not a works program.

But prayer does enter strongly into the development of my relationship with God:

- In prayer I come to learn more about God's person
- In so doing I will discover the beginning of His nature infusing my nature with His
- I will find healing in His presence

- I discover self-understanding while with Him,
  as
- I search my own heart, my own motives and
  my own thoughts.

I best learn about Him before His Throne and I best learn about me while I'm with Him. Time in His presence, therefore, is not earning time, it's learning time.

Begin with Worship

So it was, when I heard these words, that I sat down and wept, and mourned for many days; I was fasting and praying before the God of heaven. And I said: "I pray, LORD God of heaven, O great and awesome God, You who keep Your covenant and mercy with those who love You and observe Your commandments."[1]

Nehemiah's opening words express the delicate balance in understanding which tunes our hearts with God's. He extols God's greatness and His mercifulness at once and together; the enormity and the tenderness of God is viewed simultaneously.

We need to grasp this balance.

Always keep God's grandeur, His majesty and His awesomeness in view. But the objective in doing so is not to cultivate a theology or to become intimidated. Viewing and extolling the enormity of your Father will settle your confidence in His sufficiency for your need. He is bigger than life: He is therefore able to handle your life! Yes, God is transcendent beyond all worlds, but He is also within earshot of your feeblest cry. He has a "covenant of mercy" with you—just because you love Him!

Committed to Obey

> I pray, LORD God of heaven, O great and awe-
> some God, You who keep Your covenant and
> mercy with those who love You and observe
> Your commandments, . . . O Lord, I pray, please
> let Your ear be attentive to the prayer of Your ser-
> vant, and to the prayer of Your servants who
> desire to fear Your name.[2]

Notice in this prayer the close relationship between loving God and obeying Him. The emphasis is on the heart—
on the one who loves Him and is intent on doing what
pleases Him. "Your servants who desire to fear Your name
. . . who love You and observe Your commandments."[3] God
honors such a desire, and hope and confidence should rise if
you understand the spirit of Nehemiah's prayer. He had not
attained perfection, but he prayed with a *heart* of obedience
and God answered him.

I have spoken with thousands of people who view their
present failures as guarantees God will never be able to
complete His purpose in their lives. For these people—
indeed for most of us—a call to obedience seems a virtual
seal against victory, for perfect obedience eludes them. But
again, note the link this prayer forges between the heart and
the intent to obey. What counts more is what I *want* than
what I *am*.

First Samuel 16:7 says, "Man looks at the outward
appearance, but the LORD looks at the heart." He clearly is
not as concerned with our perfection as He is with our
direction. The praying heart that is intent on obedience may
not immediately perfect those intentions, but God is set to
respond to that one according to his "heartset."

Confession in Prayer

We have acted very corruptly against You, and
have not kept the commandments, the statutes,
nor the ordinances which You commanded Your
servant Moses.[4]

For God's will to be realized in my life, rather than my
own way, I need to be sensitized toward my sin. When I
confess my sin, the Holy Spirit will help me become (a)
unhooked from the clutching power of past sins and (b)
unharnessed by the sin that would seek to find present
expression through me.

We have been damaged enough by sin's impact. Let us
confess what we perceive as sin and ask for Holy Spirit
insight to see all the more perfectly what sin may still
remain in us.

I recently found myself feeling uncomfortable about a
practice in my own life which I knew to be perfectly and
biblically allowable. It involved my viewing habits with television. It wasn't as though I was watching impure pro-
gramming. I wasn't. Nor was it that I was watching more
often than before.

What was at issue, as the Spirit probed the possibilities
of growth, was my recognizing a new value He was placing
on my time; His call to a deeper sense of its use. My privilege was to continue my schedule; His call was to reevalu-
ate it. And the longer I procrastinated, the more I came to
see the wasted time as "sin"—not a damning failure, but a
sense that I was missing something better that God had for
me.

As a result, I trimmed my televiewing time (He didn't

require I omit it altogether), and I found real joy in the gain realized through accepting this discipline. But it started by seeing the self-indulgence as "sin." The Holy Spirit reproved me of the sin of waste and summoned my confession. I had taken a pure liberty granted to me as a believer and, by reason of attitude, had turned it into a license for selfishness. Confrontation by the Spirit and confession in prayer has helped me avoid future waste in that aspect of my life and opened the path to growth in another.

The Word in Prayer

Nehemiah's prayer is grounded in his understanding of the Word of God. He quotes the promises of the Word and his words are drenched in the Spirit of the Word: "Remember, I pray, the word that You commanded Your servant Moses."[5] Then he freely quotes excerpts from Leviticus 26 and Deuteronomy 4 and 28. His affirmations of God's almightiness and awesomeness are more than theological. He is referring to a God who has manifested His power in history. Nehemiah's familiarity with the record of God's workings is at the root of his faith as he prays. He also quotes those portions of the Word that affirm God's loving-kindness and mercy.

Similarly, the Holy Spirit wants to bring the Word of God to mind as we pray to lead us beyond mere humanistic ideas about God.

Praying according to the promises of the Word reminds us that it is His nature to be good, loving and merciful, so your prayer needn't be concerned as to what His will might be. He's revealed it. His nature is to save, to heal, to rescue, to redeem, to provide and to answer! The truths of God's Word says so, and by feeding upon it we will soon find its truth and the faith it brings filling our praying.

Bring Your Requests

"Let Your servant prosper this day."[6] Nehemiah specifically adds his request for royal favor when he goes to speak with the king about spending a term of duty away from the palace. He is direct in his request, but it is beautifully and wisely worth noting that the petition comes after he has taken four steps:

1. Viewed the greatness of God in worship
2. Expressed a desire to obey God
3. Been renewed in contrite confession
4. Reviewed God's Word with promise.

Rebuilding the human personality is undertaken from a stance on your knees and the Holy Spirit will assist you in doing so. Just as Nehemiah's words have instructed us in its manner, so the Spirit will help our weaknesses when we cannot know how to pray as we should.[7]

The building process will involve your complete partnership with Him and prayer is the foundational meeting point for that partnering. He will not do the job for you, but is present to help the task to be accomplished in you. Daily "executive planning sessions" will advance the project, so meet with this Highest Level Helper and pray.

"But you, beloved, building yourselves up on your most holy faith, praying in the Holy Spirit[8] . . . . Praying with all prayer and supplication in the Spirit[9] . . . . For the Spirit helps our weakness . . . making intercession for us with unutterable groanings . . . interceding according to the will of God.[10]

Notes
1. Nehemiah 1:4-5
2. Nehemiah 1:5,11
3. Nehemiah 1:11,5
4. Nehemiah 1:7
5. Nehemiah 1:8
6. Nehemiah 1:11
7. See Romans 8:26-27.
8. Jude 20
9. Ephesians 6:18
10. See Romans 8:26-27.

CHAPTER SEVEN

What Holiness Is Really About

*Joy is the discovery that everything
you dreamed true fulfillment would be
has already been planned for you by God
Himself, and that He is ready to
bring it about—for you and in you.*

—J.W.H.

"And it came to pass in the month of Nisan, in the twentieth year of King Artaxerxes, when wine was before him, that I took the wine and gave it to the king. Now I had never been sad in his presence before. Therefore the king said to me, 'Why is your face sad, since you are not sick? This is nothing but sorrow of heart.' Then I became dreadfully afraid, and said to the king, 'May the king live forever! Why should my face not be sad, when the city, the place of my fathers' tombs, lies waste, and its gates are burned with fire?' Then the king said to me, 'What do you request?' So I prayed to the God of heaven."
Nehemiah 2:1-4

A S OFTEN AS THE WORD "holy" is used by Christians, you would think that all agreed on a uniform understanding of its meaning. We have "Holy" on our Bibles, announce plans for partaking of "holy" communion, sing "Holy, Holy, Holy" and, all in the same breath, acknowledge the "Holy" Spirit—Third Person of the Godhead. By reason of these usages, "holy" seems generally to mean "divine" or "of God."

Then the word of "holiness" enters a conversation, a discussion among Christians, and there it may vary from the title for a hierarchal church clergyman to the observance of a ritual standard of behavioral requirements. In this usage "holiness" can mean anything from the Pope to teetotalism; from a bishop to not-wearing-makeup.

Then the theologians begin: "Holiness" is defined as an attribute of God or the perfection of Christ's nature or the justified believer's position in Christ or the sanctified believer's manner of living. The word in some form—holy, holiness, holiest, hallow, hallowed—occurs nearly 700 times in the English Bible—sure it's important!

But what do *you* think it means? What does the word "holy" or "be holy" or "you are called unto holiness" suggest to you?

The average believer seems to feel threatened by the idea of holiness. He tends to see it as describing something of God's unapproachable side or as demanding a quality or standard of life which he feels is beyond him. Holiness tends to be defined by "feel" more than by fact, and the feeling seems to be, "Boy, that's way beyond me (although I sure want to try my best!)."

What the Holy Spirit Is up To

Our study in Nehemiah's mission—his concern, compassion and commitment to help the people—is designed to help us understand the Holy Spirit's desire to bring each of us to complete personhood. This practical pursuit—our partnering with Him as He comes to help—is geared to make us *whole* or *holy;* for that's what "holiness" is really about—*wholeness.*

> What the *Holy* Spirit is up to is
> to bring the *whole* life of Jesus Christ
> into the *whole* of our personalities
> so the *whole* love of God
> can be relayed to the *whole* world.

The "whole idea" is "holiness." And by looking in on Nehemiah, we can gain a workable definition of holiness and grasp its practical application for us.

Chapter 1 concludes with a calling card introducing Nehemiah's conversation with King Artaxerxes. It informs us of his office as cupbearer; a position which was more than a mere servant, but one which at times involved a consultant role—an advisor of sorts. It was this status that gave Nehemiah his favored access to the emperor.

The text gives us some informative insights into the customs and atmosphere of an ancient royal court.

Remember, Artaxerxes is a pagan king—a monarch ruling the 127 provinces of the Persian Empire, stretching from the border of China on the east, to the Mediterranean on the west, including Egypt and Asia Minor. The privilege and power of such sovereigns often manifest in impulsive and unpredictable behavior; in flights of passion and bursts of fury. So, we can understand Nehemiah's fear when the king inquires as to the reason for his sadness. Custom required that anyone allowed in the king's presence radiate his/her sense of privilege, but Nehemiah's grief over the report from Jerusalem, coupled with his extended period of fasting with prayer, were so preoccupying that he was guilty of violating accepted protocol.

"Why the frown?" Artaxerxes demands, noting his cup-bearer's gloom.

Nehemiah's instant response combines three beautiful traits: practical sensitivity, bold assertiveness and spiritual wisdom.

He *pacifies* the king: "O King, live forever!!" (A discretionary greeting when the present possibility is the lopping off of your head!)

He *presents* his case: "My forefather's city is wasted."

And he *prays* to God; a good example of the scriptural propriety of brief, pointed, emergency prayers which "find grace to help in the time of need."

The ensuing conversation results in Nehemiah's assignment to the task of rebuilding Jerusalem's walls. But before we study the significance of all that the king commissions and provides for, look at the passion which motivates Nehemiah. There's something about it that reflects the essence of the Holy Spirit's nature and concern for us.

The whole of this passage, beginning with Nehemiah's response to Hanani's report, to his intercession and tears, through to his risking his life in allowing his deep, troubled concern to be seen in the king's presence—all this unveils the character of a person who cannot be content until those he loves are satisfied.

That is at the heart of the nature of God.

If there is anything which summarizes the meaning of the Holy Spirit's mission to earth, it is His reflection of the Father's desire that everyone come to know the life and the love He has opened for the whole world to share. Though it is God's holiness that man's sin has violated, it is also His holiness—His very *Spirit* of holiness that He has sent into the world. His holy purpose is to restore—to wholly rebuild—just as Nehemiah's concern was for complete reconstruction.

Nehemiah's words to Artaxerxes are neither demeaning nor mocking toward those inhabiting Jerusalem, though long before now they should have launched the task of rebuilding. Instead of faulting the Jerusalemites before the king, he shows understanding for them and offers to do everything he can to transform their condition. In this context the Holy Spirit shines forth—the *true* Spirit of God's holiness. Nehemiah wants something done and he wants it done *now*. And in this light, the meaning of God's call to complete holiness can be heard—His desire for our full sanctification. But what does that mean, really?

Because both terms—holiness and sanctification—have become smothered in religious verbiage or suffocated by legislated programs of mandated standards, a considerable dismantling of unscriptural notions is needed for many of us. We must untangle the twisted talk about "holiness" if *holiness* is a goal God has for us, and if full *sanctification* is something I should truly desire. It obviously requires my understanding. I'm not likely to really hunger or thirst for something I don't understand, feel intimidated by or have distorted in definition. Let's get at the meaning of "holy."

In detailing the three-part nature of man—spirit, soul and body—we earlier read Paul's prayer for the Thessalonians:

Now may the God of peace Himself sanctify you
completely; and may your whole spirit, soul, and
body be preserved blameless at the coming of
our Lord Jesus Christ.[1]

In the very words of that same prayer are three statements
about sanctification or holiness. It is helpful and encouraging to note that holiness, or full recovery of spirit, soul and
body,

    1. Is for now
    2. Is something God will do Himself in us
    3. Involves peace, completeness and wholeness.

In short, God's program of sanctification means He is ready
to do everything He can to put me fully together today!

This prayer holds a tremendous promise: "May the God
of *peace* . . . sanctify you." The essential idea of the word
eirene (peace) is *unity;* of fragments or separated parts
being brought together. The relevance of the promise is
obvious, whether we are viewing Jerusalem's broken walls
or observing someone with a broken heart. Into both scenes
a Comforter has been commissioned and committed to
bring wholeness from brokenness.

The Idea of "Holy"

The full and releasing idea in God's program for our
becoming "holy" deserves understanding. I think it would
help if our own English word "holy" were better defined to
our thinking. This word "holy," as used today, is derived
from the medieval English *hal,* an eleventh-century word
which is the root to such contemporary words as "health,"

"hale," "whole" *and* "holy." This fact evidences the truth
that the conceptual meaning of holiness is more than a spiritual attribute; it relates to more than just the invisible. Holiness involves the entire, broader idea of *wholeness*—of
completion in all parts of the human being. Take all three
aspects of you, for example:

- Your spirit can be revived to life in God (made
  holy)
- Your soul can be restored in mind and emotions (made whole)
- Your physical body, habits and conditions can
  become disciplined and recovered to well-
  being (kept healthy).

Holiness becomes a far more practical and desirable
goal when seen in the light of its fuller meaning. And the
Bible is clear that *all* of these things are God's objective in
making us holy. He isn't merely trying to produce stained-
glass people or plaster-cast saints who work to satisfy some
religious criteria. He wants you to become holy—complete
in all your being—just as *He* is holy.

Holy as He Is Holy

The phrase, "be holy as He is holy," requires study, for
what to many of us may seem a prohibitive summons or
unattainable goal actually gives us a glimpse into the
Father's heart and desire for us.

It is in Leviticus that this high call is initially issued:
"For I am the LORD your God. You shall therefore sanctify
yourselves, and you shall be holy; for I am holy."[2] For years
that verse caused me to shudder with a dubious, reverential

fear that would sweep my soul. Reading the words, I knew I was accountable to their summons, but I also felt that they held an obviously impossible challenge.

Compounding my sense of concern, and deepening my fear of failing, I noted Jesus saying essentially the same thing: "Therefore you shall be perfect, just as your Father in heaven is perfect."[3] Here was an Old Testament and a New Testament summons calling me to be perfect. A paralyzing sense of helplessness and hopelessness would possess me: "I want to be what you want me to be, Lord, but it all seems so out of my reach." A divine call intended to beget hope produced fear and condemnation instead. And I never really gained ground until, through simple understanding, that futile sense of being a "failure-before-you-start" was broken.

Before we go any further, can we establish that? If the walls of your personality are going to be rebuilt, you need to come to the same place of comfort and confidence that God's Word gave me. Let me elaborate.

Two Kinds of Holiness

I know of nothing that hinders the pursuit of holiness more than a sense of condemnation. Guilt, unworthiness and the feeling of impossibility about ever being truly satisfying to God war against faith and hope. But both these rise when we discover the two ways holiness and perfection (to which the Lord calls us) are revealed in His Word.

First, see that your holiness is initially secured before God by virtue of your *position* in Jesus Christ. In other words, when you received Christ Jesus as Saviour, you were made "positionally" holy. That means Jesus' sinless record was credited to your account. The Epistle to the Romans often uses the word *justified,* a word which means that God has made a legal judgment about us when we trust in Christ. By the standards of the Highest Court in the universe, He regards us as *holy*—perfect because Jesus *was* perfect; and in Him we are totally declared "not guilty" of *any* sin. Because the flawless record of Jesus Christ is superimposed over our failures, God says, "Wholly holy!"

Second, God's Word talks about holiness in *practice*. He wants you to get on with a life that is *lived* "holily," which *practices* holiness in thought and conduct. This means He expects growth in practical holiness, while He in the meantime accepts us as positionally holy. It's beautiful to feel the peace of His love sustaining our position in His sight while we're growing. But He won't allow us to neglect responsible growth in practical holiness on the grounds we are already positionally holy. It was learning to see and to balance these two facts that broke my fear and allowed me to really hear what the Lord Jesus was saying in the words, "Therefore you shall be perfect, just as Your Father in heaven is perfect." I had long held this as solely a commandment, but I came to see it was actually filled with a promise. He was saying, "Because your Father is holy, you are assured already that you are enroute to holiness."

Let's elaborate even further. How vividly this can bring hope to our hearts!

Two Steps to Confidence
There are two steps which I am convinced can bring a settled confidence to anyone that God can make them holy.

Step One: To understand holiness in God's changeless nature;
Step Two: To understand His promise about your new nature.

First, let's understand *holiness* as it applies to God. Holiness, by actual definition, is that attribute of God by which He preserves the integrity of His own being. This means that God never needs to be reminded to be good, loving, wise or wonderful. He does not say, "I'm going to be nicer today" or "I hope I don't do something evil." In other words, He doesn't labor to accomplish that which most of us define as "being holy."

Instead, because God's very nature *is* "holy," it means He will never be less than what He is already. That is, His holiness guarantees the changeless integrity of His own being.

> He will never be without love for you.
> He will never be less than merciful.
> He will never be other than just.

He will never be *anything* other than what He is by the glorious essence of His very being, for His "holiness" is that which preserves the whole perfection and completeness of His Person.

But in contrast to this is Man. First created in God's holy image, but now unholy as the result of the Fall, Man has been shattered, smashed and damaged; reduced to far less than he was made to be.

But it is here, at this point, that God's salvation enters the scene. And His entrance is not only to forgive Man but to restore him. The plan is to birth Man all over again, and through this new birth to place in him a *new seed*—a new genetic principle in human nature. We are to be "born again, not of corruptible seed but incorruptible, through the word of God which lives and abides forever" (1 Pet. 1:23).

But the implications of this promise elude many. While God's very own Word makes a promise concerning the certainty of this "new seed" potential, our doubts (due to our fears and failures) sustain a misunderstanding.

I know it did with me.

But what first involved a misunderstanding, I later came to understand as a promise from God about my new nature. My joyful discovery sprang from a passage once causing doubts about my experience with God. First John 3:6 and 9 say,

> Whoever abides in Him does not sin. Whoever sins has neither seen Him nor known Him . . . . Whoever has been born of God does not sin, for His seed remains in him; and he cannot sin, because he has been born of God.

I used to read those verses and be ready to give up.

I would say to myself, "Well, I *think* I'm born of God, but this says if you are you don't sin. But sometimes I still do. I don't want to, but I do. I mean, I love the Lord and I'm trying to become more holy, but I still sin."

Then the words of verse eight would haunt me: "He who sins is of the devil."[4] Doubt and futility would grip me: Since I'm not sinless yet, am I really saved?

Years went by and no one ever told me differently. Like many, repeated trips to altars and prayer rooms seemed to be the only way to assure God's acceptance. But one day I learned that the verses which had confused me actually contained a beautiful and mighty truth.

My misunderstanding was overcome simply by discovering a Greek verb tense. I learned that the original language actually says, "Whoever is born of God *does not keep on sinning.*" I had thought it meant, "whoever is reborn *never* sins," but it didn't. As a matter of fact, the immediate context acknowledged *both* our call to purity and our fallibility:

> My little children, these things I write to you, that you may not sin. And if anyone sins, we have an Advocate with the Father, Jesus Christ the righteous. And He Himself is the propitiation for our sins, and not for ours only but also for the whole world.[5]

Don't sin. But if you do, His blood is your covering! What a truth for us who want holiness though we still sin!

So I learned the Bible was *really* saying this: "Whoever is born of God . . . does not keep on sinning." That is, he doesn't make as good a sinner anymore—he won't keep at it the same way he did before! The message is also this: The seed of His new life in me assures me that my destiny is to conquer sinning. His life in me makes me unhappy when I sin as I did in the past.

How often, before you knew Christ, did you sin and feel justified in doing so? Remember feeling free to retaliate, to let your temper flare or to serve yourself selfishly? Have you noticed since your rebirth that an inner sense of wanting to please God has begun to predominate? Do you experience a greater sensitivity toward His holy will prevailing? The reason is this: What is born of God can't keep on sinning, *for His seed remains in him.*

God's seed is in you! He says, "I birthed you into *my* life, and therefore, the attributes of my personality shall be forthcoming in you." Let me illustrate this truth.

Becoming Like Father

As any picture of or contact with me reveals, I have a receded hairline. Now, as you can imagine, I did not plan to be balding. In my early twenties I did not make a decision, "I think I'll start losing hair."

But I did begin losing it. And anyone could have predicted it would happen. Both my grandfathers and my dad had precisely the same hairline and the same genetic principle that caused them to be balding was transmitted to me. My brother and I have patterns of baldness similar to our forebearers. The biological genetic—the seed transmitted to us—predestined that this trait would be present.

But, oh, can you see?

This rather silly illustration points out how God is saying to you and me, "My seed is in you, and since *I* am holy, you are going to be increasingly so." We shall be holy for He is holy. We shall become perfected just as our Father in heaven is perfect. Holiness—His holy nature—is progressively going to fill my broken, weak and damaged parts. The character and constancy of my Father will grow in me—His child.

And Nehemiah said, "Send me that I may rebuild," to which the king replied, "How long will your journey be?"

"And I set him a time." Nehemiah registered his request[6], and do you know for how long?

One of the most moving things in this whole book is to discover that he asked for 12 years!

I can imagine a man asking, "May I have a two-month leave of absence?" or "Well, King, sire, I would like the opportunity to be there. Well, could I possibly have a year?"

But 12 years?!

Just as Nehemiah recognized the task would not be

accomplished rapidly, the living God has sent His Holy Spirit to work completeness in you—even though it takes time.

And just as the king agreed, so it is today: "The Lord will perfect that which concerns me; Your mercy, O Lord, endures forever."[7]

Whatever time it takes, He is committed to your completion, and that completed work will be a work of holiness unto the Lord—worked in you by the Holy Spirit of God.

Notes
1. 1 Thessalonians 5:23
2. Leviticus 11:44
3. Matthew 5:48
4. 1 John 3:8
5. 1 John 2:1-2
6. See Nehemiah 2:5-6.
7. Psalm 138:8

PART TWO

Dimensions of Development

*Jerusalem's walls, how can it be I see
your stones arise?
If this can be, then surely thus can God
restore our lives.*

*Come, Holy Spirit, have Your way,
O Comforter Supreme.
Rebuild my soul, redeem all loss, fulfill
my highest dream—the Father's purpose.*

—J.W.H.

CHAPTER EIGHT

Building Supplies and Project Plans

*But Isaac spoke to Abraham his father and
said, . . .
"Look, [here is] the fire and the wood, but
where is the lamb for the burnt offering?"*

*And Abraham said, "My son,
God will
provide for Himself the lamb
for a burnt offering."
And the two of them went together . . .
and . . . called the name of the place,
"The-Lord-Will-Provide."*

Genesis 22:7-8, 14

"Then the king said to me, 'What do you request?' So I prayed to the God of heaven. And I said to the king, 'If it pleases the king, and if your servant has found favor in your sight, I ask that you send me to Judah, to the city of my fathers' tombs, that I may rebuild it.' So the king said to me (the queen also sitting beside him), 'How long will your journey be? And when will you return?' So it pleased the king to send me; and I set him a time. Furthermore I said to the king, 'If it pleases the king, let letters be given to me for the governors of the region beyond the River, that they must permit me to pass through till I come to Judah, and a letter to Asaph the keeper of the king's forest, that he must give me timber to make beams for the gates of the citadel which pertains to the temple, for the city wall, and for the house that I will occupy.' And the king granted them to me according to the good hand of my God upon me. Then I went to the governors in the region beyond the River, and gave them the king's letters. Now the king had sent captains of the army and horsemen with me." Nehemiah 2:4-9

WHAT IS NEEDED for the rebuilding of a personality? How is the job contracted? What materials are needed? Are there permits to be issued, as a city code might require for a projected structure?

These aren't only interesting questions, they're necessary ones. They sharpen our sense of the truth that rebuilding the real you is not just a play on words—it's a real project. It will take real time and will require real materials. As Nehemiah requests of the king a leave of absence from the court, the reality and practicality of planning for reconstruction unfolds in our text.

Artaxerxes is as quick to respond favorably to Nehemiah as he was quick to show displeasure over Nehemiah's despondency. Apparently God answered Nehemiah's prayer. The king immediately changes his demeanor and he and the queen willingly hear Nehemiah's request. And all the more moving—especially in light of our comparative study—is to see the evidence of Nehemiah's forethought and preparedness.

He is ready for the occasion.

He instantly seizes the opportunity and makes his requests known. He has planned carefully for this moment, and in his specific requests, we are provided insight into principles that help us find the best answer to the question: What is needed to rebuild a personality? In the basic things for which Nehemiah made appeal, truth unfolds from which personal comfort can be gained.

Nehemiah requests and is given four things as he obtains the right to pursue the Jerusalem rebuilding project.

They are:

1. *Time*—an extended period of leave from his
   duties at the palace
2. *Authority* to enter the region of activity
3. *Resources* for the actual building project
4. *Troops* to secure his mission and support him
   in the event of opposition.

Each of these items apply to our own program of personal renewal. But before we examine the nuggets of truth in these four gifts, let's take a minute to assure that one preliminary issue is settled. It involves an important distinction in personal spiritual experience.

Bondage and Captivity

In discussing the process of restoration in the human personality, we need always to distinguish rebuilding from rebirth.

You have probably been born again already. Your interest in this book is probably but one evidence of your sincerity and desire to grow as a Christian. But I have wondered if another possibility might be the case for you. Can it be that as you have been reading, you have become aware of something unsettled in your own soul? A longing, perhaps, that seeks an established confidence about your personal relationship with God?

If this is so, it is further possible that until now you have never actually come to a specific moment in your life when you asked Jesus Christ to be your Saviour. Have you ever personally invited Him into your heart?

We all need to do so, you know.

Jesus said that unless we come to God in humility as

children, we cannot truly begin in the life of God's Kingdom.

> Assuredly, I say to you, unless you are converted and become as little children, you will by no means enter the kingdom of heaven. Therefore whoever humbles himself as this little child is the greatest in the kingdom of heaven.[1]

Let me ask you gently, but pointedly: "Have you ever done that?"

Have you knelt humbly as a child and confessed your sin to God with childlike honesty? Have you prayed with childlike simplicity, inviting Him as the young child's song requests,

> Into my heart, into my heart,
> Come into my heart, Lord Jesus?[2]

If you haven't until now, then would you—now join me in doing that? Just pray *now*—simply, quietly, but speaking these words with sincerity:

> Holy Father God,
> Depending on Jesus, I come to ask your forgiveness for all my sin.
> I want your will in my life and your Word as my guide.
> Thank you for giving your Son for my salvation:
>   I now believe in and receive Him as my Saviour and as my Lord.
>   I receive your love given to me
>   through His death on the cross, and

> I receive your life given to me
>> by His resurrection from the dead.
> Lord Jesus Christ, come into my heart.
> Fill me with your Holy Spirit,
>> and let all my tomorrows increase in your way
>> from here to eternity. Amen.

Let's pause a minute. Whenever the moment that transaction between you and God occurred, whether just now or years ago, together, let us stop right here and praise God!

The fact of Christ's entry into our lives is an ever present reason for praise. You and I have *great* reasons to lift our voices with praise full of thanksgiving. Here are just seven!

1. *All our sins are forgiven completely!*
   God says, "Their sins and iniquity I will remember against them no more."[3]

2. *Complete peace with God has been established!*
   "Being justified by faith, we have peace with God through our Lord Jesus Christ."[4]

3. *The courts of heaven resound with joy because of our salvation!*
   Jesus said there is joy in heaven over each sinner who repents.[5]

4. *Our names are now written in the Book of Life!*
   It is an actual registry in which God has listed all of us as His redeemed.[6]

5. *We have an absolute hope of eternity in heaven!*

   "The gift of God is eternal life through Jesus Christ our Lord."[7]

6. *Christ promises His daily presence and provision!*

   "I will never leave or forsake you . . . I have come to give life abundantly."[8]

7. *God has committed Himself to help us resist evil!*

   "And if God be for us, who can be against us? . . . We are more than conquerors through Him."[9]

Go ahead and do it! Rejoice and praise with great thanksgiving!

Lift your head.
Lift your hands.
Lift your voice.

New life in Jesus Christ is yours forever, and these seven facts are only a few of the multiple guarantees you have from God—promises which secure confidence for your future. And it is beautifully assuring that hereby God's Word gives firm footing for tomorrow. Whatever yet needs recovery, you have a solid and sufficient foundation in Christ. Here are grounds for rejoicing and upon which you can progress with rebuilding!

Two Distinct Points of Beginning

Pausing to insure your foundation in Christ is important simply because without our rebirth, rebuilding is an impossible task. Without secure footings through faith in the death and resurrection of the Lord Jesus, any attempts at building or rebuilding a life are destined for frustration and failure. "No other foundation can anyone lay than that which is laid, which is Jesus Christ."[10]

However, once our *beginning* is secured in Christ, *building* can be effectively pursued. It is therefore, not surprising that the Bible delineates so clearly between foundations and rebuilding. In a real sense *both* are a beginning, but each is distinct and needs understanding. Thus, God's Word not only teaches two distinct points of beginning, but there are Old Testament parallels to illustrate each of the two.

The initial beginning point is regeneration: "You must be born again."[11] We've just outlined that point at which the foundation is laid. It is virtually instantaneous, because everything about it has already been accomplished for us through Christ's death and resurrection: we are saved completely by His grace and His work[12] and secured in the power of His perfected salvation for us.[13]

The second beginning point is sanctification:[14] "He who has begun a good work in you will keep performing it until the day Christ returns for you."[15] This is a progressive program of growth and involves our responsible partnership with the Holy Spirit. It includes the Lord's promise to restore to us all that we have seen lost or destroyed in our past.[16]

So the two points merge. When the initial "beginning" is established—rebirth—we're ready for the second—rebuilding. Look at the examples in Israel's history. On two ancient occasions the Jews found themselves troubled by circumstances in lands distant from their Promised Land of God's intended purpose.

The first was their sojourn in Egypt. After Jacob's family relocated, during his son Joseph's influence there, later rulers reversed what had been a benevolent setting. The Israelites' situation progressively deteriorated until later generations were put under slavery. Centuries later, under Moses, came their exodus, when the Lord delivered them, saying: "I have brought you out of Egypt, out of the house of bondage."[17] Through the miracle of the Passover and the mighty display of their passage through the Red Sea, they were liberated; a nation resurrected from death.

The second was their exile in Babylon. Following Jerusalem's destruction, the Jews were made political captives—a displaced people "marking time" as it were. But when the quota of prophesied years-of-judgment was fulfilled, the Lord brought them back, returning them to the land of their inheritance and the city of their former rule.

Now there is a vast and obvious difference in these two experiences. It's an instructive difference, much like the distinction between regeneration and sanctification— between being reborn and being rebuilt.

For example:

1. In *Egypt* they were slaves under brutal task-masters. In *Babylon* they were refugees, but with the opportunity of carrying on some-what of a normal enterprise.

2. In *Egypt* their slavery was simply the result of their heredity. After successive generations each one was simply born into bondage. In *Babylon* their exile was the direct result of

sinning which produced their situation. They
were a destroyed and displaced people.
Furthermore, the pathway to release in each case was different:

- Deliverance from Egypt came through the
  blood of the Passover lamb.
- Return from Babylon came by means of the
  king's edict, according to the prophecies of
  God's Word.

The relevance of contrasting Israel's Egyptian bondage
and Babylonian captivity is that the rebuilding process we
are studying parallels the outcome of the latter event—their
return from exile. That must be clearly seen because we
should never suppose a person's new birth is a process—it
isn't.

Our rebirth in Christ is a crisis, a moment in time when,
like Israel's deliverance from Egypt, the blood of "the
Lamb of God who takes away the sin of the world"[18] is
acknowledged. That is our only hope of freedom from sin.

But following this we will all come to that time we
begin to deal with the fruit of past disobedience, in the same
way Israel's exiles returning from Babylon had to face the
charred remains of Jerusalem which was the direct result of
past sinning.

First, the Lord Jesus Christ comes as Saviour—the only
solution to our deadness in sin, our lostness from and our
guiltiness before God. His cross is the key to our redemption and His resurrection power the key to our receiving the
gift of new life in Him.

Second, the Holy Spirit comes as Comforter—the One

sent to assist us in our helplessness, to instruct us beyond our ignorance and to recover us from all our brokenness. His power is promised us and His leadership given to assist us forward in our new life for Christ. He comes with all the equipment needed for our rebuilding, renewing and recovering.

Some thrilling analogies to our experience are highlighted by an analysis of the text before us.

The Need for Letters of Authority

> Furthermore I said to the king, "If it pleases the king, let letters be given to me for the governors of the region beyond the River, that they must permit me to pass through till I come to Judah."[19]

Analysis: Each of the Persian Empire's 127 provinces was ruled by a satrap—a provincial governor charged with protecting the emperor's interests and the empire's boundaries. Customs were due, passports required, documents checked and the usual requirements of at least a cursory investigation of all travellers was administrated. In Nehemiah's case an unusual need for evidence of his mission and commissioning authority was needed, for upon arrival he would be functioning under a special order of the king's court. Although his mission would not completely displace the regional governor's authority, it would alter its dimension. Insofar as the Jews and Jerusalem were concerned, Nehemiah was invested by Artaxerxes with a higher authority than Sanballat, the satrap over the region. Nehemiah was governing with direct authority from the emperor. His request for documents indicating his right of passage and privilege of rule are understandably requested. It will greatly expedite the task if there are no questions as to who's in charge.

Analogy: When Jesus ascended to heaven, He had expressed at least two promises of far-reaching significance: (a) He would build a Church and (b) He would give the Church authority to act in His Name.[20] He further made clear that the Holy Spirit's coming would provide the power to accomplish the task of building and the ability to exercise the power of His Name.

And the Holy Spirit has come!

As participants in His building process, we need to understand the authority the Spirit has brought us. The Comforter wants us all to utilize the letters of authority we have been given: "Whatsoever you ask in my name," Jesus said, "the Father will do it for you . . . . [21] All authority has been given to Me in heaven and on earth . . . . "[22]

These credentials—the privilege of praying and operating in the name of Jesus—are the letters of authority pressed into your hand by Christ the King. The Holy Spirit will teach you to function in those rights as well, and this is a significant point of learning because we are all a people living on a planet under contest.

Since man's fall, the Adversary, like a Persian satrap, is ready to claim authority unless we can verify higher claim. And that's what we have been given in Jesus' name. We not only have throne rights of *access* to God, we have throne rights to *advance* Christ's kingdom IN HIS NAME!

Just as Sanballat's authority over Jerusalem and its residents was preempted by Nehemiah's letters (see Neh. 2:20), so the Holy Spirit has come to enforce the King's orders concerning you. Whenever the devil seeks to drop a pall of gloom over you, distressing you with a spirit of heaviness—whenever he seeks to encroach upon the present workings of God's purpose is your life—drive him off the property: "You have no authority here! In Jesus' name I declare my right to freedom and privilege of pursuing God's project in my life!"

Materials for the Project

And a letter to Asaph the keeper of the king's forest, that he must give me timber to make beams for the gates of the citadel which pertains to the temple, for the city wall, and for the house that I will occupy.[23]

Analysis: The crucial need for wood in the ancient day cannot be appreciated by today's building standards. So many varied construction materials are now used, and steel is so commonly utilized for frames and beams in large structures, that we can easily miss the significance of Nehemiah's request. He needed the large timbers for structural framework. They would be absolutely essential for the completion of the project.

Notable, however, is the fact that the vast majority of the material to constitute the rebuilt walls will be the stones that are already on the site. They will use tons of rock— some stones still the shape originally quarried and others broken beyond apparent use—but all of it remaining debris of the former walls.

Analogy: In the conjoining of these two materials— new beams and old stones—there's a picture of God's redemptive program which restores broken people like us. First, there are always things which God must bring to our recovery. Paul seems to hint at this supply-line ministry of the Holy Spirit in his letter to the Philippians:

> For I know that this will turn out for my salva-
> tion through your prayer and the supply of the
> Spirit of Jesus Christ . . . . My God shall supply
> all your need.[24]

The Holy Spirit's *supply* is foreshadowed in Nehemiah's request for those materials which must be brought to the task; those "timbers" of God's resource for renewal which He is more than ready to provide.

But, like the broken, fallen stones of Jerusalem's wall, there are also things present within you which, though battered by the past, can be readied again for building. There are traits of your own unique personality, memories of your own past, qualities of your own character—distinct hallmarks of You—which God wants repaired and retained: "For it is God who works in you both to will and to do for His good pleasure.[25]

These two resources provided by Nehemiah—authority and materials—forecast the method God is using to equip us by the ministry of His Holy Spirit today:

1. The Adversary is confronted with our badge of authority: Jesus' Name!
2. The task is approached with sufficient resources: a renewing supply of divine grace and a redeeming power to recover building blocks from broken pieces.

And with all of this, as the text describes, Nehemiah was given a cordon of soldiers—another mighty point paralleling the Spirit's ministry to us.

What do those soldiers represent today?

Notes
1. Matthew 18:3-4
2. Harry D. Clark, *Into My Heart*. Public domain.
3. See Hebrews 10:17.
4. Romans 5:1, *KJV*
5. See Luke 15:7
6. See Luke 10:20
7. Romans 6:23, *KJV*
8. See Hebrews 13:5; John 10:10.
9. Romans 8:31,37
10. 1 Corinthians 3:11
11. John 3:7
12. See Ephesians 2:8-9.
13. See Titus 3:5.
14. There is an actual sense in which we are viewed as holy (sanctified) at the time of our regeneration; but all Scripture notes that this position we are given by faith is intended to summon our growth *into* that gracious acceptance God grants us *while* we are growing.
15. See Philippians 1:6.
16. See Joel 2:23-29.
17. See Exodus 20:2.
18. John 1:29
19. Nehemiah 2:7
20. See Matthew 16:17-19.
21. See John 14:13-14, *KJV*.
22. Matthew 28:18
23. Nehemiah 2:8
24. Philippians 1:19; 4:19
25. Philippians 2:13

CHAPTER NINE

A Band
of
Angels

*"Don't bother me," the collegian said, "I
haven't time for religious nonsense and the
efforts at counting how many angels can dance
on the head of a pin!"*
*"I won't any longer," said his pastor,
"when you can escape the memory of the one
who saved your life when you were six years
old."*

—J.W.H.

"Then I went to the governors in the region beyond the River, and gave them the king's letters. Now the king had sent captains of the army and horsemen with me. When Sanballat the Horonite and Tobiah the Ammonite official heard of it, they were deeply disturbed that a man had come to seek the well-being of the children of Israel."
Nehemiah 2:9-10

THE BELOVED SPIRITUAL intones, "Swing low, sweet chariot . . . a band of angels comin' after me,"[1] and sentimentalizes on the presence of angels at the time of death. There *are* "a band of angels" mentioned in the Bible. Jesus said He could have, at will, summoned a host of them to rescue Him.[2] But the angels of Scripture are neither playful cherubic dolls or "chariot" attendants at death. Even though the Bible has much to say about angels and their role toward us, a dearth of teaching about them exists.

There are some who have so reacted to superstitious ideas about angels that they seem to take exception to the truth on the subject. But religion's hangover from medieval traditionalism is no threat when we heed the Word.

Paul wrote to the Colossians, "Let no one defraud you of your reward, taking delight in false humility and worship of angels."[3] His warning to not become preoccupied with the subject of angels is soundly in view, but it was never intended to remove us from an understanding of their activities. There are, in fact, as many references to angels in the New Testament as in the Old—almost 300 in all! So let us address the theme wisely, giving an appropriate emphasis to a subject which can be as imbalanced by neglect as by preoccupation.

Angels and You

First, Hebrews 1:14 says, "Are they not [angels] all ministering spirits sent forth to minister for those who will inherit salvation?" That's an extremely important verse because it pointedly has us to understand that angels are not merely winged wonders flitting around in the sky, but are ministering spirits appointed an explicit task. They are assigned ministry toward "those who will inherit salvation."

Now the Bible makes clear who this is: We are salvation's heirs, all the redeemed in Christ. Romans 8:16-17 says, "We are . . . heirs of God and joint heirs with Christ." And in Ephesians 1:11 we read, "In whom [Christ] also we have obtained an inheritance." It is no exaggeration of the Word to accept the fact that included in the vast benefits and promises of the great inheritance God gives us, He has provided the attending ministry of angels. He has sent "a band" of them to assist us and to work at His direction in our behalf.

Remember the Acts 12 account of Peter being freed from prison? An angel loosed him from his cell and caused sleep to fall on the guards.[4]

Remember in Acts 8 when Philip left Samaria to go to the desert to meet a man in need? An angel told him to do that.[5]

Remember in Acts 12 (after he killed James), when Herod smugly arrogated authority to himself and suddenly dropped dead under divine judgment? An angel struck him down.[6]

Remember in Acts 27 when Paul was storm-tossed aboard the ship bound for Rome and he urged all on board to take heart because God assured him of their safety? An angel delivered that message to him.[7] "Are they not all ministering spirits sent forth to minister for those who will inherit salvation?"[8]

The biblical answer is yes! Here are clear New Testament cases of angelic agents assisting people of the kingdom with deliverance, guidance, comfort and judgment.

Yet someone might say, "Those cases are certainly true and quite remarkable, but those things just don't happen today—except, well, in some Communist country or something." But the eternal Word declares "For He [the Lord] shall give His angels charge over you, to keep you in all your ways. They shall bear you up in their hands, lest you dash your foot against a stone."[9] Angels have the ministry of *protecting;* that's at least one of their assignments.

Most of us can point to times when something unexplainable suddenly happened—imminent disaster was averted or remarkable deliverance effected. And all of a sudden we recognize it—the Lord sent help! Some of the most phenomenal stories I've heard in my life, miraculous stories of invisible but obvious assistance, are apparently the activity of angels. Intellectualism taunts those who suggest the possibility of contemporary angelic action, but it isn't fanatical to believe such things occur. We might well let the Word open our eyes to see.

Most of us see into the invisible realm with great difficulty. But there is more activity there than some suppose. In 2 Kings a marvelous story involving angels is told.[10]

During the time of the prophet Elisha, the king of Syria sent a large military contingent of horses and chariots—a great army—after him. When Elisha's servant saw the enemy surrounding them he cried out, "Alas, my master! What shall we do?" Elisha's calm response has become a classic quotation: "Do not fear, for those who are with us are more than those who are with them."

The wise old prophet not only knew he had divine protection—he *saw it.* When his servant responded by saying, "I don't see any troops on our side," Elisha prayed, "Lord, open his eyes that he may see." And God opened the servant's eyes to see that "the mountain was full of horses and chariots of fire all around Elisha."

This promise is yours as well. God provides *accompanying* care as well as the protective, the liberating and the ministering work of angels. He has "sent forth [angels] to minister" for us.

The captains of the army and horsemen that accompanied Nehemiah beautifully parallel the ministry of angels in the life of the believer. They aren't to be sought or worshiped, but they have been assigned and we needn't fear acknowledging their activity. Just as armed troops accompanied Nehemiah from the palace in Shushan, so God, in pouring His Holy Spirit upon the Church, has also bequeathed provisionary troops—the hosts of the Lord, a band of angels to assist us when need arises.

The Fallen Ones

But this is only one side of the coin. In stark contrast to the angelic hosts serving the Father's purpose are dark powers aligned against us: "For we do not wrestle against flesh and blood, but against principalities, against powers, against the rulers of the darkness of this age, against spiritual hosts of wickedness in the heavenly places."[11] Sanballat's opposition to the efforts on Jerusalem's walls reflect the satanic, tyrannical nature of our Adversary, the devil, who is set against our wholeness:

> When Sanballat the Horonite and Tobiah the Ammonite official heard of it, they were deeply disturbed that a man had come to seek the well-being of the children of Israel.[12]

Sanballat was the provincial governor over the realm of

Judah and his control had been absolute. Previously nothing could happen without his approval. But now one fact overruled that: Nehemiah had brought official letters from the emperor putting the Jews in Jerusalem under Nehemiah's authority. He had been given the right, if he wished, to annul anything Sanballat said. It was the one hope that these citizens had for realizing the restoration of their city walls.

Now we read that this spiteful ruler *grieves* that a man has come from the king to help these oppressed and needy people.

Think about it! It is so characteristically satanic!

Sanballat's only interest is to keep the people in a state of defeat and despair, for his sole purpose is to secure rule over them. He exacts taxes from them, concocts demands of them and exploits their weaknesses. He is completely disinterested in the well-being of these he has been charged by the government to serve. Sanballat's spirit is as accurate a picture of Satan as you will find anywhere in Scripture.

Facts About the Devil

The prophets Isaiah and Ezekiel both speak about the fall of Lucifer.[13] Under the configuration of the *prince of Tyre*, Satan is identified as a sinister being, destructive in every design, hideously hateful and opposed to all that is God's purpose and desire.

In Genesis he is introduced as the *serpent* in the Garden, the same title that follows him into the book of Revelation where he is also called the *dragon*.[14] He is primarily referred to as *Satan* (meaning *accuser* and *adversary*) and "the *devil*" (meaning *slanderer*). The Bible reveals that Satan is a spirit being who was originally created in beauty and perfection by the hand and breath of God, but who rebelled against the Most High. Still, as a created being, he is finite in his capacities, though he transcends the power of mankind in our present estate.

Though he is a formidable adversary, Satan is not omnipotent, however great his power. Only God has *all* power. And Satan is not omnipresent—only God can be everywhere. Through demon hordes, which like an evil army serve at his direction, the devil seeks to strategize and execute his master plan—a program formulated to deceive and destroy individual persons and the whole race of mankind as well.

It is important to know these facts about the devil, for contrary to the notion that he is only an abstract force, a negative way of thought or an impersonal expression of evil, the Bible gives a different picture. God's Word reveals him as a distinct, vile personality who rules the forces of darkness and operates systematically in the spiritual realm against everything good, righteous, noble, pure and healthy.

Satan Is Our Adversary

Just as Nehemiah knew how to deal with Sanballat by leading the Jews in resisting his efforts at hindering them, we need to let the Holy Spirit's message in the Word unmask Satan's person and methods.

First Peter 5:8 calls him our adversary and teaches us to "be sober, be vigilant; because your adversary the devil walks about like a roaring lion, seeking whom he may devour." Some sincere believers are intimidated by such words and prefer to simply skirt the subject and pretend their enemy will leave them alone if they do the same with him. But that idea is unjustified. The Word *says* he is stalking us. So let's learn the truth about him and allay all fears.

Concerning Satan's powers, certain reasonable questions rise.

First, how broad is Satan's arena of action? The God we worship and the Christ who redeemed us both created and rule the entire universe! Satan's scope of power is only on this planet, earth. That may be small comfort, however, since this is where we live and his assault seems unavoidable. But before we faint or tremble, remember it is also to this small planet that God has sent His Son and announced, "All authority has been given to Me in heaven and on earth."[15]

When Jesus offers the privilege of being born again into God's Kingdom, the fact is that new birth places each of us outside Satan's realm of rule, even though we continue to live on this planet where the battle still rages for human souls. Perhaps it will help us to grasp the nature of this battle if we understand its history, for man was not originally placed on earth in this dilemma.

How did Satan gain rule over this planet? According to the Bible, God created our planet for man's governorship under God. But through deceit and disobedience, man believed and obeyed the serpent's lie. He listened to the snake, disobeyed the Creator, and thereby, Satan has come into controlling management of the earth—a role originally intended to be man's. The devil still exercises this rule by "just rights," having received license to this rule through man's disobedience to God and his forfeiting his God-given rule to Satan. We know the devil has legal claim to function on earth, for when he offered "all the kingdoms" of this planet to Jesus, attempting to seduce Him to sin, Jesus did not contest the devil's right to make that offer. He did rebuke the temptation, but He didn't correct the tempter's right to make the proposition. Thus, the struggle goes on to see man's rule reinstated under God. So, understanding the history of the battle, the next logical question is:

What license does Satan have to operate in my life? The entire life of a person outside of Jesus Christ is lived under the sway of the prince of the power of the air, "the spirit who now works in the sons of disobedience."[16] In other words, an unregenerated person not only is still in his sins because of Adam, but he is also completely vulnerable to the dominion of the Adversary by reason of living in his domain.

This certainly does not mean that every unbeliever is demon-possessed. Nor does it necessarily mean that non-Christians even consciously or willfully serve Satan. But it does mean that man's whole thought system, his whole pattern of life and conduct, is far more motivated, animated and manipulated by the Adversary than he understands. The whole world, the Bible says, is under the influence of the Evil One.[17]

And how shall I recognize and respond to Satan's workings? There are several traits of his activity. *Satan is a liar,*[18] but you don't have to respond to the lies of the Adversary. *He is an oppressor,* but you don't have to let him oppress you. Keep Acts 10:38 in mind: "How God anointed Jesus of Nazareth with the Holy Spirit and with power [to deliver] . . . all who were oppressed by the devil." That's just one of the sure promises we live in as the same Holy Spirit is present to help us!

Satan also infects hearts and minds with evil. Jesus likened the Adversary to a sower of evil seed that grows into a weed-filled garden,[19] who directs activity sowing things opposing God's goodness in your life. He further seeks to steal the good seed of the Word of God when it comes to us. He will resist faith-inspiring promises and fruit-bearing seed,[20] but you can counterattack by clinging to and declaring God's Word of truth! Don't let the thief succeed at stealing, killing or destroying.[21]

Now summarize these satanic traits:

- He lies
- He imposes fear
- He depresses
- He sows doubt
- He seeks to defeat and discourage.

Where good things have begun, he'll seek to abort what God's Word is working. When the Word does gain a foothold, he seeks to snatch it away. As your enemy, he'll seek to wipe out any and all hope of holy, joyous expectation.

But remember that although we live on the scene of this conflict and face these devilish devices, don't allow that fact to suggest surrender. You have your rightful place in God's promise and victory! Our Nehemiah has come with letters of authority that overrule our opponent and preempt his authority over us!

Truth will overthrow his lies.

Deliverance will cast out his oppressive works.

The work of grace will weed out what he seeks to sow.

Anything that opposes you has an answering counterforce in God's Word, and the Holy Spirit will stir your mind and warm your heart and faith. Though the thief comes to steal and destroy, the Holy Spirit will rise with Christ's abundance of grace so that your restoration and growth can go on: "When the enemy comes in like a flood, the Spirit of the LORD will lift up a standard against him."[22]

Victory is *yours! Now!*

And yet I have sometimes felt the soul-wearying hostility of hell wearing me down. Amid the struggle I have felt low at times, even though I knew I was destined for triumph beyond the test. If you've ever felt like that, wearied though you're winning, maybe this story will help you as it has me.

Playing "Away from Home"

When I played basketball in high school on one occasion we were playing "away"—playing a game on another school's home court. Our team was playing quite well—outscoring the opposition, in fact—but somehow the sense of winning just wasn't there. Our momentum began to fade. Recognizing the problem, our coach called "time." As we huddled at the sidelines, he began. "Hey guys, listen up. You're *winning*. But I know it just doesn't 'feel' like it. Now brace yourselves. Understand this. You're playing on 'enemy territory' and you've got little crowd support."

Because of the distance, few of our high school's kids were there. The crowd was made up of opposing fans. Every time we'd score, we heard nothing but boos. Whatever the other team did was lauded and applauded, and though we were ahead, a horrible sense of being defeated hung in the air. The coach recognized its effect on us, and having wisely helped us see the source of our "lag," he sent us back into the game.

We won.

And so it is in the middle of some trying situations. The Adversary opposes you. You're in God's will and purpose, but sometimes feel depressed: "It sure doesn't *feel* like I'm winning!"

But cheer up, Teammate!

Don't let the Adversary's crowd of demon liars get you down. We may not have the home court advantage at this time, but we do have the presence of a Coach who wants you to remember, "He who is in you is greater than he who is in the world."[23]

Yes, Sanballat will continue to prove to be a hatefully accurate picture of Satan. And in Nehemiah, we will further see a very tender picture of the Holy Spirit confronting evil and advancing the recovery process. In helping you withstand the Adversary, the Holy Spirit further assures you,

- "I'm going to get you together"
- "I'm going to rebuild you"
- "I'm going to restore you."

Dear one, there's overcoming confidence in perceiving the real nature of the spiritual battle. The enemy and his company are real, but so is the conquering Comforter and His heaven-sent troops.

Everything Satan can do can be overruled by the present ministry of the Holy Spirit in you. Let the Holy Spirit make the letters of authority in God's Word alive to you and in you. Overrule the devil and stand in the certainty, "that He who has begun a good work in you will complete it until the day of Jesus Christ."[24]

I may be uncompleted, but I'll never be defeated.

Notes

1. Traditional Negro spiritual. Public domain.
2. See Matthew 26:53.
3. See Colossians 2:18.
4. See Acts 12:4-10.
5. See Acts 8:26.
6. See Acts 12:20-23.
7. See Acts 27:23.
8. Hebrews 1:14
9. Psalm 91:11-12

10. See 2 Kings 6.
11. Ephesians 6:12
12. Nehemiah 2:10
13. See Isaiah 14:12-15; Ezekiel 28:11-19.
14. See Genesis 3; Revelation 12.
15. Matthew 28:18
16. Ephesians 2:2
17. See 1 John 5:19.
18. See John 8:44.
19. See Matthew 13:24-30; 36-43.
20. See Luke 8:12.
21. See John 10:10.
22. Isaiah 59:19
23. 1 John 4:4
24. Philippians 1:6

CHAPTER TEN

Breaking Loose from Condemnation

The next time the devil comes to remind you about your past, remind him about his future.

—Anonymous

"So I came to Jerusalem and was there three days. Then I arose in the night, I and a few men with me; I told no one what my God had put in my heart to do at Jerusalem; nor was there any animal with me, except the one on which I rode. And I went out by night through the Valley Gate to the Serpent Well and the Refuse Gate, and viewed the walls of Jerusalem which were broken down and its gates which were burned with fire. Then I went on to the Fountain Gate and to the King's Pool, but there was no room for the animal that was under me to pass. So I went up in the night by the valley, and viewed the wall; then I turned back and entered by the Valley Gate, and so returned." Nehemiah 2:11-15

ONE OF THE TENDEREST and loveliest verses in the Bible is from the often-quoted twenty-third Psalm: "He leads me beside the still waters. *He restores my soul.*"

This faithful gentle description of our Saviour's ministry is but another reminder of God's purpose to *restore*—to recover whatever remains wounded or broken in us. This next piece of history Nehemiah describes provides mighty truth which unmasks another adversary to our fullest development: condemnation.

Few things are more crushing than it is. The soul-wrenching power of condemnation has proven how emotionally and mentally crippling it can be. It wipes out one's sense of God's peace and plays havoc with faith's underpinnings. But Jesus' loving attention, as our soul-restoring Good Shepherd, wants to lead us beside the streams of Holy Spirit-inspired truth and the liberating rivers which can dissolve the chains condemnation has forged.

Nehemiah's restoration work in Jerusalem is so representative of the way the Holy Spirit begins His restoration work, it's unsurprising so many vivid analogies occur.

There were 10 gates to the ancient city of Jerusalem before it was destroyed. Nehemiah mentions in 2:11-15 visiting the ruins of three of them: The Valley Gate, the Refuse Gate and the Fountain Gate (see App. A). The purpose of this tour, which Nehemiah took before anybody even knew why he had come to Jerusalem, was to see what the actual condition of the walls were. His survey is to study where he will first need to concentrate his efforts. His report notes that as he proceeded, he finally came to a place he could go no further. The destruction of years before had been so complete that the rubble blocked his passage at every turn. He specifies a point on the severe eastward slope where the ruination made it too dangerous to advance any farther. He turned back and reentered the city by way of what remained of the Valley Gate—the point he had earlier exited. Nehemiah's survey report gives both a sense of the devastation and an appreciation for the enormity of the task he faced.

We are studying actual events in history and yet we discover in them so many devotional analogies. Types break forth everywhere, picturing redemption and showing how the Holy Spirit works today. As we trace this man's survey of ruins, notice the phrase, "after three days." It's the first of several points at which you'll find parallels quite helpful in breaking free from condemnation's quest at quenching the joy of the Lord in your soul.

Analysis: Nehemiah's arrival at Jerusalem was followed by three days of virtual inactivity. There was no fanfare, no high celebration, no announcement of intent. The passage of time was doubtless a practical one of adjustment, of his getting settled following the arduous demands of so extensive a trip. These days would also have provided time for thoughtful consideration of his first steps, now that he had actually reached the scene of his mission.

Analogy: How often have you wondered why God doesn't do things more quickly? Since impatience with God's "waiting periods" is trying for the most mature, how much more is it true of those who have yet to learn that the coming of the Spirit rarely includes an immediate change of circumstance?

Over the years I have had many ask, "Pastor, since I've been filled with the Holy Spirit, I *feel* different but it doesn't seem like much else *is* different." They go on to note how a week . . . two weeks . . . a month has passed, and they're concerned that dramatic events aren't filling their days "like all those" they've heard testify.

I usually seek to comfort them with two facts:

1. My experience with dramatic testimonies is that they are honest, but usually abbreviated. People report, in condensed version, things which took much longer in coming about. Don't feel like a second-class Christian when time seems to be passing by and action seems slow.

2. God is never in a hurry. Yes, the presence of the Holy Spirit within us does bring an instant witness; He's there and He's at work.[1] But remember this: The gifts and the fruit of the Spirit aren't unwrapped with haste or grown at a moment's notice. If things aren't happening fast, you're normal.

The relevance of our learning to recognize that God's delays are not denials is that such understanding can defuse the tendency to feel unworthy—condemned—simply because things aren't happening as fast we think they would if we were "more acceptable" to God.

Analysis: Nehemiah makes a triple reference to his nocturnal tour investigating the condition of Jerusalem's walls.[2] He was not yet ready to tell the people his plan, nor was he interested in the provincial government knowing his purpose. So under the cover of darkness, silent in their exit and quiet about their task, a small group of men traversed the devastation caused by a disaster occurring a century and a half before. Even as the people slept, unaware that long-sought help had come and lifelong embarrassment would shortly be overcome, Nehemiah went about his task, dedicated to their interests.

Analogy: How apparent the Scriptures are that God is always awake and alert, tending to our need: "The God of Israel never slumbers or sleeps"[3] and "I lay down and slept; I awoke, for the Lord sustained me."[4] His Word indicates that even while we are at rest, our Father's program for our blessing is being sustained. As surely as your heart is kept beating through the night, His heart concern for you is being carried out.

Sometime back, through the death of a family member, I was moved to do a study on God's activities "in the dark." I was amazed at the number of major events in the Bible that brought victory in the midst of darkness:

- Creation's light sprang into the darkness of chaos—Genesis 1
- Jacob wrestled all night and gained a new identity—Genesis 32
- Israel's Passover deliverance took place in the night—Exodus 12
- Gideon's battle unto victory began in midnight hours—Judges 7
- Jesus' cross was immersed in inky blackness though it was midday—Luke 23.

Even when Jesus comes again it will be as a thief "in the night"[5] and during an era of history predicted as one in which "darkness shall cover the earth and deep darkness the people."[6]

This truth can bring such bright exhilaration to the soul! The Holy Spirit is ministering to your need *now*. Whatever the apparent darkness, God "never forsakes the work of His hands."[7] Rather than allowing the darkness of waiting or depression to become a shadow of doubt or letting a cloud of questioning cause you to believe yourself the victim of God's apparent inactivity, learn this wisdom.

Dark times are intended for your *rest*. When they come, lean back and recline in the everlasting arms of the Almighty. Allow the Holy Spirit to work *out* and *through* what He's surely at work doing.

I guarantee when morning comes you'll be surprised!

Lessons at the Valley Gate

Analysis: Nehemiah's survey team exited at the Valley Gate passageway from Jerusalem. This gateway, like all the others, was now only a worn path, not a structure. It seems more than coincidental that this is the first point of reference.

Interestingly, the Valley Gate derives its name from its view upon and access to the small, narrow Valley of Hinnom (see Appendix A). Long before Nehemiah's visit and far earlier in Jerusalem's history, the Canaanite people had worshiped there. Human sacrifices had been offered as their satanic ritual was pursued.

Later in history, at a time the Hebrew prophets confronted Israel for involving themselves in the same evil rituals, blood and death still stained and shadowed Hinnom. Eventually the people were judged and exiled for reasons including the fact that some had sacrificed their children in this very valley. It had been a shrine of Baal; the damning cult that defied God's laws and pled the evil case for perversion (see Jer. 32:35). Thus the Valley of Hinnom became known as the Valley of the Flame or Fires; a place where human sacrifices had been offered. Even when this period passed, Hinnom still continued to be used as a place for burning rubbish; a fact prompting this valley's adoption as a symbol of forthcoming horror. Both in the book of Revelation, as well as in Jesus' preaching, an ultimate site of eternal damnation is described. Gehenna (a form of the name Hinnom) is that awesome, awful lake of fire.

Analogy: Clearly, the Valley Gate's prospect is a ready and logical picture of hell, for it depicts the prospect of a life outside Christ, with neither hope nor meaningful destiny. And it is not profane to observe that one's present life, if outside of God's will, can be "a hell of a life"—hellishly self-centered, hellish in its activity, hellish in its fruit and hellish in its destiny. What the Valley Gate represented from Israel's past is symbolized in our study. It's the point where the worst of the past is seen and where it is dealt with conclusively.

Valley Gate—Lookout to the Past

That Nehemiah's first survey exits from the Valley Gate parallels the Holy Spirit's desire to start by begetting in us a personal sense of our past having been dealt with. Here is His invitation to you and me: "Stand at the doorway of your life and look on your past. Its future was eternal loss. Just as the Valley Gate faced the western, sunset side of the city," the Spirit continues, "see yourself secured in Christ's forgiveness—the sunset declaring an end to that segment of your life." Standing at Jerusalem's gates, in confidence that yesterday has concluded, brings a fresh certainty concerning my tomorrows. On the cross Jesus declared, "It is finished!" confirming the completeness of all salvation. Now the Holy Spirit makes it personal: "Whom the Son sets free is free indeed."[8] You never need to account for the past again!

The Serpent Well

Analysis: The viability of the Valley Gate being analogous to the securing of our souls is highlighted by the fact that nearby this gate was the Serpent Well. Nehemiah mentions it and it is still marked today.

Scholars say the Serpent Well was named in the way folk names have always been ascribed to geographic sites today. Just as Indians and settlers have given such names as "Devil Mountain" or "Snake Creek" for logical or superstitious reasons, the Serpent Well was probably named for the fact that a snake had been found and killed there at some time in the past.

Analogy: The image is graphic: A thirsty man seeking water is attacked by a snake coiled at the well. The snake is slain and the man's thirst slaked. In this beautiful picture we can hear Christ say, "Whoever drinks of the water that I shall give him will never thirst. But the water . . . will become . . . a fountain . . . springing up into everlasting life."[9] Thirsty souls respond. Yet, just as the Serpent would seek to prevent access to this joy, so the Son of God has risen to smite the Serpent's head. And now He calls us to drink endlessly at the well of salvation's joy.[10] In Nehemiah's starting through the Valley Gate and coming to the Serpent Well, envision a picture of the Holy Spirit wanting to bring us to:

1. A place of security about our past
2. A place of victory over the devil's efforts at depriving us of daily joy of our salvation.

The Holy Spirit would say, "I want to bring you to a well where you will drink with joy and rest without fear; where the serpent is pressed under your feet and my dominion rules in your life. You are no longer subject to the accusations of the liar concerning any aspects of your past sin and failure."

Steadfast confidence in your relationship with God is basic to feeling confident about the future. The Holy Spirit wants to help you with this. If God was sufficient to cover your past, when you were dead in sin and lost from His purpose, He can handle your future now that you are one of His own.

Break free from condemnation!

Whenever the enemy accuses you, learn to resist his efforts in the resource of God's truth. Stand your ground on what God has spoken about your sins:

> If we confess our sins, He is faithful and just to forgive us our sins and to cleanse us from all unrighteousness (1 John 1:9).

> As far as the east is from the west, so far has He removed our transgressions from us (Ps. 103:12).

> Who is a God like You, pardoning iniquity and passing over the transgression . . . . [You] will again have compassion on us, and will subdue our iniquities. You will cast all our sins into the depths of the sea (Mic. 7:18-19).

> "Come now, and let us reason together," says the LORD, "though your sins are like scarlet, they shall be as white as snow; though they are red like crimson, they shall be as wool" (Isa. 1:18).

> I have blotted out, like a thick cloud, your trans-
> gressions, and like a cloud, your sins. Return to
> Me, for I have redeemed you (Isa. 44:22).

> Then He adds, "Their sins and their lawless
> deeds I will remember no more" (Heb. 10:17).

That last verse, which quotes from Jeremiah 31:34, declares one of the mightiest possibilities in the universe. God forgets sin. "Their sins and their lawless deeds I will remember no more." He means this! It is not a case of senile forgetfulness, but of divine eradication. He completely removes our sin record from His memory. In other words, God says, *"Because my sinless Son's record of righteousness is now applied to you, and because I have no instance of sin to recall about Him, I can't think of anything you've done that displeases me!*

That's what being justified means. We are acquitted of any grounds for judgment. We now stand with Christ before the heavenly tribunal and the Almighty Father God, judge of all, says, "I have superimposed my Son's record over yours. Now, I regard you as never having sinned. Your past is abolished from my memory."

Live in this confidence, loved one. Rejoice in condemnation-free living. And the next time the devil comes to remind you about your past, remind him about his future!

Notes

 1. See Romans 8:14.
 2. See Nehemiah 2:12-13; 15.
 3. See Psalm 121:4.
 4. Psalm 3:5
 5. See 1 Thessalonians 5:2.
 6. See Isaiah 60:2.
 7. See Psalm 138:8.
 8. See John 8:36.
 9. John 4:14
10. See Isaiah 12:3.

CHAPTER ELEVEN

Two Gates
and a
Miracle

*Are you looking for the fullness of
the blessing of the Lord,
In your heart and life today?
Claim the promise of the Father, come
according to His Word,
In the blessed, old-time way.*

—C.H. Morris[1]

"Then I went on to the Fountain Gate and to the King's Pool, but there was no room for the animal that was under me to pass. So I went up in the night by the valley, and viewed the wall; then I turned back and entered by the Valley Gate, and so returned. And the officials did not know where I had gone or what I had done; I had not yet told the Jews, the priests, the nobles, the officials, or the others who did the work." Nehemiah 2:14-16

THERE ARE FEW QUESTIONS more often asked than those by Christians wondering: What's the holdup? How can I get moving? How can I rise above the things that cripple me? My friend, Lane Adams, has succinctly expressed this feeling in the title of his book, *Why Is It Taking Me So Long to Get Better?*

Amazing numbers of believers seek miracles to resolve the problems that cripple their progress. They want Jesus to speak an immediate word: "Rise and walk." How we would all like our growth and rebuilding to be accomplished with but a word. Yet the Saviour says instead, "I'm going to *teach* you to walk rather than *cause* you to, for far greater things are learned when you discover a walk *with* me and not just a miracle *from* me."

This process is very much like the natural one by which a child learns to walk. It begins with the child's natural desire to want to get up—to gain a beginning capacity to stand on its feet. Next he will learn to move about while still holding on. Then, having learned healthy balance, he eventually steps forth to the joyous delight of the whole family.

There are miracles involved in our learning to walk in the life of the Spirit of God, but they aren't completely essential to that walk. There are basics we must start with and then, at times, miracles will follow. But first steps are usually slow in coming, and the miracles are joyful moments rather than a continuum of phenomenal events.

When our oldest son was born his feet pointed almost

directly outward. At first we all thought this would gradually remedy itself. But by the time he was beginning to scramble around and pull himself to his feet, nothing had changed. As he began to walk it was with difficulty. He could not walk well and there was sufficient cause for us to take him to the doctor for attention and treatment. For months special shoes were placed on him and it appeared the next step was leg braces, for still no improvement occurred.

This is one of the most precious stories in our family history and my wife Anna tells it best. She had just left one doctor's office for another. The first, who had been caring for little Jack, had recommended the baby be fit with braces and given therapy by an advanced specialist. Anna had just boarded the bus en route to another specialist that morning and, with the baby in her lap and her hands grasping his feet, she simply prayed, "Lord Jesus, you know how much I would like this little boy's feet to be all right." That was the entire prayer! Yet minutes later, as she disembarked from the bus and entered the next specialist's office, they both looked with astonishment at our son's feet—they were perfectly straight! What months in remedial shoes had not changed had been rectified by the touch of Jesus in 15 minutes! They were both dumbfounded with delight, and you can imagine the praise session Anna and I had together as we laughed and rejoiced over the genuine miracle of the instant recovery of our little boy's foot condition. What long-range implications for his future!

We still rejoice when relating that episode. It was real, unimagined and given by God's grace. And I tell it here because there is within it a principle about our learning to walk in the Spirit. Young believers, like young children, *do* have the capacity to stand, the ability to get around *and* the desire to move forward with balance. But there is still a miraculous dimension of life to which we all need to truly move forward—to run the race of a Spirit-filled life.

These "first steps" and a miracle outline the text of Nehemiah. With the two steps in the last chapter, three more are discernible from Nehemiah's first excursion. They depict further foundational points of moving forward in a Spirit-filled walk—the steps following the joy of finding condemnation-free living.

Dealing with Sin

Analysis: Older translations called this the "Dung Gate," a name it bears to this day in modern Israel. Of course, the titling of a portal using the word for human excrement is admittedly distasteful. But the fact is that daily, the city's garbage was removed through this gate and that refuse included human excrement. It is quite obvious that the Refuse Gate is a picture of the purging and cleansing process every earnest believer must walk through daily.

Analogy: There is nothing more fundamental to a healthy walk with Christ. As completely as our past sins are forgiven and our position secured in God's grace, there is still a need for maintaining our hearts in purity before Him. Being among the first places scrutinized by Nehemiah, the Refuse Gate is reflective of the Holy Spirit's aim to keep us sensitive to sin, obedient in life and conscientious to confess our sin when we fail. "But if we walk in the light as He is in the light, we have fellowship with one another, and the blood of Jesus Christ His Son cleanses us from all sin."[2]

I have sometimes found it difficult to talk with people about sin and their own need for keeping sensitive to confess and keep cleansed daily. So many individuals quickly feel utter condemnation. It seems as soon as one says anything about sin a giant self-destruct button is pressed and condemnation clouds their countenance. But in dealing with us more deeply to prompt holiness of life, Christ does not point sin out to condemn us. He's revealing it so we will repent, confess and be brought to a new place "in the light." There is cleansing, confidence and joy available as the blood of Jesus Christ purifies and delivers.

This daily need for confession is similar to the body's breathing process. As we inhale, oxygen is carried to the bloodstream and courses throughout the whole body. In circulation, the blood picks up impurities from cells throughout the body and upon return the impurities are filtered through your lungs—some even expelled with exhaling. So it is when the Holy Spirit surfaces sin. He is not accusing, "Ah-hah, I *see* you!" as though some heavenly helicopter was spotlighting your failure until angelic officers arrive! But He does use the light of the Word to show you where He wants to deal in your life next.

Where sin is surfaced, confession is required: "If we confess our sins, He is faithful and just to forgive us our sins and to cleanse us from all unrighteousness."[3] The combination of the Word and the blood of Jesus Christ will work their way through your whole spiritual system, beginning to purify all you'll allow. And as you confess (somewhat as exhaling in the circulation process) your confession of sin becomes the key to freedom.

The Greek word for "confession" is *homologeo*. It means, "to speak the same thing." That is, to say about sin what God is saying to you about it. Confession involves being honest, forthright and not excusing yourself either to God or to your own conscience. If the Father says, "I don't want you to do that," then respond, "Lord, I don't want to do that." If He says, "I see that you have not yet surrendered that," then say, "I see it now Lord, and do surrender it." Confession: I say what He says and the light of His Word (with the cleansing power of the blood of Christ) progressively purifies me.

The same passage in 1 John reminds that if we say we have no sin, we're fooling ourselves. Remember, the position we have gained in Christ is not threatened. Peace is not sacrificed during this process of practical sanctification. But your total acceptance before the Father is no substitute for the fact that He is calling you to move into holiness—that is, restoration and a fuller wholeness of personality.

We can't be any more accepted than we already are as His children.

We can't be any more victorious than we are in the dominion He's given us over the power of the enemy.

But we can become progressively purer in the practical details of daily living.

Balance these truths and move ahead. The Dung Gate is part of the program. And as disturbingly graphic as the picture is, the message is clear: Daily purging is no shame; it's healthy.

Being in the Word
"Then I went on to the Fountain Gate."[4]

Analysis: Most scholars believe that the Fountain Gate was given its name because its eastward location was just above and opened to a path leading down to the Kidron Brook (see Appendix A). It would have been the gate through which many of the people went daily in order to get water.

Analogy: The Fountain Gate seems to readily depict the Word of God. The Bible describes itself in many ways: as bread, milk, gold, honey, a mirror, a hammer, and in John

15, as water. Jesus said, "You are already clean because of the word which I have spoken to you."[5] As the people went daily to get fresh, life-sustaining water at the Fountain Gate, so it is impossible for a believer to survive apart from continuous interaction with the Word of God. If you were to ask me what a believer needs in order to move on with God, I would say that a believer needs to:

1. Know where he stands with God in Christ
2. Know He has been given dominion over the devil in Jesus' name
3. Know how confession of sin allows an ongoing, purifying work of the Spirit
4. Know that he needs to be in and daily feed on the Word
5. Know that he is to be filled and live in the fullness of the Spirit.

The Fountain Gate illustrates the fourth point, just as the King's Pool does the fifth.

Being Full of the Holy Spirit

Then Nehemiah says, "I went on . . . to the King's Pool."[6]

Analysis: The King's Pool resulted from a project initiated approximately 300 years before Nehemiah's time. About 750 years before Christ, Hezekiah, one of Judah's godly kings, rose to power. Among his building projects was the strategic carving of an underground conduit designed to bring a fresh water supply into the city of Jerusalem. Until that time, whenever Jerusalem was attacked by enemies, a simple siege could reduce the people to defeat. But now, thanks to Hezekiah, the solid granite conduit brought water from the Gihon Spring outside the city walls to a pool built within the city (later named The King's Pool). It was a remarkable engineering accomplishment for any time, but all the more considering the conduit was dug 2,700 years ago! It is an interesting archaeological fact that the workers started from opposite ends and cut their way through the rock to within one foot of a precise contact.

When the King's Pool was dedicated, it meant that a continuing life-saving water supply was now within the city of Jerusalem. Some scholars suggest that Psalm 46 was penned to be sung at the celebration of that pool's inaugural: "There is a river whose streams shall make glad the city of God" (v. 4).

The King's Pool was functional in Jesus' time (and still is today!) and was called the Pool of Siloam. Remember when Jesus put mud on the blind man's eyes? He said, "Go, wash in the pool of Siloam,"[7] and the record indicates that the man born blind began *seeing*.

Analogy: The biblical record of the King's Pool gives a picture of a *flow*—a water supply *within* that:

1. Helps to resist attack
2. Sustains refreshment
3. Ministers healing.

Nothing could more beautifully bespeak the purpose of being *filled* with the Holy Spirit!

As I mentioned earlier, our son's first steps were significant. But the miracle healing of his feet was the mighty, much-needed release of his walking, even *running,* into his future.

And I now urge personal application of that message.

Assurance in Christ and *dominion* over the serpent: we

studied these concepts at the Valley Gate and Serpent Well.

Confession and *growth* in the Word: we saw these analogies at the Dung and Fountain Gates.

But now, King Jesus wants to open a flowing stream of fresh, living water by the fulfilling of His promise to you: "You shall receive the gift of the Holy Spirit!"[8]

To His promise of salvation's "fountain of water springing up into everlasting life"[9] Jesus adds the offer of His Spirit's "rivers of living water flowing from within you."[10]

Jesus wants you to be filled with the Holy Spirit. Here is a resource of power, flowing from an unending source. "Spirit-fulness" can alleviate your thirst, strengthen you when you're under attack, provide refreshment through daily prayer and praise in the Spirit and can release a flow of Christ's healing power through you to others.

Ask Jesus to fill you with the Holy Spirit. Praisefully come into His presence and by faith receive His promise: "The promise is to you!"[11] Expect His miraculous touch upon you as He answers your hunger and thirst.

After you have been filled, keep a fresh walk in Spirit-fullness. Ephesians 5:18 literally reads, "*[Keep on being]* filled with the Spirit." Don't only say, "I'll drink at the well." But having been satisfied, keep coming daily to the King's Pool. Keep the fountain flowing in your soul!

Notes

1. Words by C.H. Morris. Public domain.
2. 1 John 1:7
3. 1 John 1:9
4. Nehemiah 2:14
5. John 15:3
6. Nehemiah 2:14
7. John 9:7
8. Acts 2:38
9. John 4:14
10. See John 7:38.
11. Acts 2:39

CHAPTER TWELVE

Knowing How God Feels About You

Beware the god your mind invents, for
you'll inevitably worship and become like him;
however wretched,
however false.
Best of all, find the true God; and
filling your mind with the truth of His
being, you'll learn His love and treasure the life
He creates.
All else is confusion. All else is ultimate
despair.

—J.W.H.

"And the officials did not know where I had gone or what I had done; I had not yet told the Jews, the priests, the nobles, the officials, or the others who did the work. Then I said to them, 'You see the distress that we are in, how Jerusalem lies waste, and its gates are burned with fire. Come and let us build the wall of Jerusalem, that we may no longer be a reproach.' And I told them of the hand of my God which had been good upon me, and also of the king's words that he had spoken to me. So they said, 'Let us rise up and build.' Then they set their hands to do this good work. But when Sanballat the Horonite, Tobiah the Ammonite official, and Geshem the Arab heard of it, they laughed us to scorn and despised us, and said, 'What is this thing that you are doing? Will you rebel against the king?' So I answered them, and said to them, 'The God of heaven Himself will prosper us; therefore we His servants will arise and build, but you have no heritage or right or memorial in Jerusalem.'" Nehemiah 2:16-20

THERE IS SOMETHING especially poignant about the mood of Nehemiah's first communication with the leaders of the Jewish community in Jerusalem. While they knew a visitor had arrived from Shushan, and they doubtless knew his respected office in Artaxerxes's court, Nehemiah himself relates to us that at this stage the officials did not know his reason for coming:

- They did not know his intent
- They knew nothing of his midnight survey
- They did not yet know the authority with which he had been endowed.

In fact, all the leaders knew, with the dawn of this conference's day, was that three days had gone by since his arrival and he had called them to a meeting.

And they met.

And in this meeting with "the Jews, the priests, the nobles, the officials, or the others"[1] of the citizenry, the disclosure of the heart of a most unusual person takes place. The remarkable sensitivity and gentleness shown by Nehemiah has to have been much of the reason he elicited such trust and cooperation from the people. Hear his first words: "You see the distress that we are in . . . let us build . . . that we may no longer be a reproach."[2]

The magnanimity of this approach is in the manner with which Nehemiah completely identifies with the people: "You see the distress that *we* are in . . . let *us* build . . . that *we* may no longer be a reproach." Except for the nature and character of this man, we can readily create another scenario.

Imagine Nehemiah as having been so affected by his high court position that he comes to the people with something like this:

> "Ah . . . hhem (self-importantly clearing his throat). I come with greetings from the emperor's palace where, as I believe you all are aware, I hold the position of cupbearer. (Dramatic pause, condescending smile.) It is somewhat awkward for me to know how best to say this. But, the fact is, I have come out of sheer frustration with the seemingly endless reports we receive in Shushan. That is, reports that you, here, have somehow, uh, not yet been able to get things in reasonable, respectable order on your own.
>
> (Now, with mild disdain.) "Feeling concern as a Jew, and with enough self-respect to disallow my being indifferent, I have come to see something done about the embarrassing state of affairs here. It *is, really,* don't you think, inexcusable that the walls are still such a mess and, of course, that the gates are in the same burned condition as when Nebuchadnezzar left town 150 years ago? Naturally I, and all of us Jews in Persia and elsewhere, are disturbed. It's difficult for us to understand why something tangible can't have at least begun before now. After all, what takes place here in Jerusalem reflects on all us Jews wherever we are.

"And so, (and I hope you can appreciate the sacrifice and the inconvenience), I have made this trip to come and provide some leadership, with orders from Artaxerxes mandating your cooperation. Naturally, I'm hoping I won't have to apply the power of my office. My letters allow me considerable authority should I need it. And I am concerned with your general and obvious lack of motivation in regards to the walls. Presuming this will change, I am hopeful of your recognizing that my time is important and the opportunity and the benefit is entirely yours. *I* don't need this work and I might well have remained in Shushan. But in hopes that my patriotism and good will toward you and the project will ignite the best in you all, I am now ready to begin. I'll be issuing orders later this week and will expect work teams to be on time.

"I'm sure you can't help but be thankful that the days of your ridiculous appearance in the eyes of neighboring peoples are shortly to conclude. If I can get what I expect out of you, I'll have this project sewed up in reasonably short order and be able to get back to Persia.

"Am I understood?" (daDA–daDA–daDA!)

This may sound and stage like cheap melodrama. It deserves to. But the pretentious manner of such self-importance is not difficult to envision—we've all seen that disgusting, patronizing spirit in someone at sometime.

Yet Nehemiah is so completely opposite to this scenario it is not only refreshing, it is beautifully instructive. His way with those he's come to help is marvelously characteristic of the way the Bible reveals God's feelings toward us—and how He wants *us* to think about ourselves.

Feeling Good About Yourself

We hear a great deal of talk today about "how you feel about yourself"—and with good reason. There are so many forces which reduce one's sense of self-worth or self-esteem, and many of us can easily feel unnecessary, unwanted and useless. Society's attempted answer for countering this syndrome is usually to mount a self-help program—an effort with either a physical, material or psychological base. Entire cable television networks exist to show you how to feel better about yourself through improving your physique, learning new skills, striking it rich with money schemes, releasing or rejuvenating your sex life, creating the new you or learning to resolve negativism, inner tension or psychological blocks. Everything is proposed from a new suit to a new spouse, from a new job to a new hobby or from group therapy to a master's degree.

As so often with we humans, we recognize need but tend to answer it with temporary measures at best and with destructive ones at worst.

It is nice to feel good about yourself and I've counselled enough people in my pastoral ministry to know how poor an image many people have of themselves. Even with the more secure among us, there is enough negative or painful input in our backgrounds that virtually none are without the need of affirmation, support, and a general, periodic message to our egos.

I'm not talking cheap flattery or manipulative lingo.

People don't need crutches for their identity; they need permanent, healing reinforcement. But human resources, however sincerely motivated or professionally administered, can never affect a completely satisfying answer for the *whole* man.

As created beings, each person has an intuitive sense of responsibility to God. Try as he might, by whatever philosophical or scientific argument, man's effort at explaining away this accountability always fails to satisfy the depth of the real hunger. "You have made us for yourself," Augustine wrote of God, "and our souls find no rest until they find it in you." Still, so many labor so diligently, yet vainly, hoping to reestablish their own personhood and self-confidence without coming to terms with their relationship to and understanding of the One who made them.

Nehemiah's sensitive approach in beginning assistance to the people of Jerusalem is important for more than diplomatic reasons. Humanly speaking, he will obviously have a much better chance at strong work relations by treating the people with respect. But the deeper issue in his style is how clearly his words and behavior reveal a true, deep-seated sense of identity *with* those he has come to help.

Here is a man who surrendered high position at the world capital, endured an incredibly demanding trip, prepared extensively to supply a multiple-year-long project, arrived with the support of royal troops and still demanded nothing of honor or deference from the Jerusalem elders. Instead he personably, gently and graciously identifies with their plight. He becomes one with them.

This style is more than humane, judicious and gentlemanly. It is divine. This is the way of the Almighty God in seeking to redeem man. It is the method of the Son of God in His incarnate approach to us all. And it is the manner of the Spirit of God as He comes to help, to heal, to strengthen and to rebuild the personalities of those Christ has redeemed.

For any thoughtful person, the most humbling fact revealed through the Bible is not our guilt before God because of our sin. Far more humbling is that the God who made us and whom we disobeyed has chosen to love us rather than damn us. An honest look at our muddle—whether personal or the entire human race—is sufficient to justify God's decision, should He simply say, "I'm tired of this tribe. Disintegrate the whole lot." If God exists, no one should blame Him if He scratched out the planet, vaporized its inhabitants and started over in some clean corner of the galaxy. But instead, "God so loved the world that He gave His only begotten Son, that whoever believes in Him should not perish but have everlasting life. For God did not send His Son into the world to condemn the world, but that the world through Him might be saved."[3]

And this love expressed itself in a way which has come to meet us where we are: "And the Word became flesh and dwelt among us, and we beheld His glory, the glory as of the only begotten of the Father, full of grace and truth . . . . No one has seen God at any time. The only begotten Son . . . He has declared Him."[4]

The whole program of God's redemption is one of loving identification with its subjects—with us. And a real understanding response to this incredible reality will form the only true basis for anyone learning to feel good about himself. When it begins to dawn upon me that God not only loves and reaches *to* me, but is unashamed to completely identify *with* me, I have discovered a foundation for recovering any lost sense of personal worth or self-esteem.

Nehemiah's words point out three things characterizing the Holy Spirit's mission to rebuild us:

- He is *compassionate* with us

- He is *committed* to help us
- He is *companioned* beside us.

Compassion: "Look at the distress we are in." The words flow with patience, are absent of criticism and pulsate with understanding. They seem to say, "Your pain is my pain. I don't see *you* as a problem, I see the problem as *ours.*"

Commitment: "Let us rise up and build." The invitation is to partnership, not servitude. The heart of God is revealed as fully set on ennobling us, the fallen. His redemption is designed to restore our joint-heirship.[5]

Companionship: "That we no longer be a reproach." What? *We* a reproach? Nehemiah had nothing to be ashamed of and neither has God. And still He comes to companion so completely with His beloved creature, Man, that His Holy Spirit breathes to our heart: "You were made in His image, and until it's restored, He considers your incompletion a reduction of His purpose. He will not rest until His character is vindicated by its fullest, most beautiful recovery in you."

It is clearly God's desire to restore *all* of you, and biblical grounds for feeling better about yourself far surpass mere psychological ones. Let's look closely at Christ's teaching on God's heart toward us: it's both strengthening and affirming.

Christ Teaches Us About God's Heart

Luke's record of Jesus' life presents a trilogy of stories He told to answer critics. Religious leaders were constantly irritated with Jesus. His teaching raised their hackles time and again as He confronted their empty notions about God.

One of their most severe bones of contention was Christ's receptivity toward people whom the religionists rejected as unworthy. "Then all the tax collectors and the sinners drew near to hear Him . . . . And the Pharisees and scribes murmured, saying, 'This man receives sinners.'"6 Following this rumble, as though to add the last straw, Jesus had dinner with a group of the religious rejects.

A dramatic tension is present here.

On the one hand, the sinful with whom Jesus met represent a hidden hope in the soul of all of us who fail. Somehow we sense that the *real* God would not abandon us because of our need, but the *religious* God seems to turn away.

The Pharisees were the personification of the latter and certainly the same spirit prevails today. But into this milieu of mixed hope and uncertainty about God's real nature, Jesus steps forth. His words answer to the secret hopes we hold, and His candor silences the Pharisee within or outside us, who shouts, "You're beyond God's point of patience! He hasn't time for washouts." And so it was that Jesus taught three consecutive parables just to show us God's heart and to give us a clear picture of how God feels about you and me.

The first parable7 is the lesson of the one lost sheep. Jesus tells of a shepherd concerned for *each* of his flock. He pictures God's heart as searching for even one person missing from among a hundred. The message is on *worth:* None of us is less important to Him because we're but one among the multitudes of humanity.

In the second parable8 Jesus describes a woman who had lost one of 10 coins. These were not ordinary coins, for in that culture they were the equivalent of an engagement ring in ours. To the woman they meant *promise*—they meant hope. The issue was more than value, it was *vision*—tomorrow's dream.

And so the woman zealously sweeps her house, looking for the lost coin—the uncompleted hope, so to speak. And upon finding it, she cries for joy, "Rejoice with me, I've found what I lost!" In this account, Jesus helps us hear God's heart as saying, "I know you feel the desire for completeness, so *know this:* You're an unfulfilled promise on my side of the ledger too. I'm as desirous of your completion as you are and I have committed myself to fulfill the dreams I've put in your heart. Since you want *me* as I do *you,* be assured—we are going to rejoice together in finding and fulfilling your deepest longings."

The third parable, the story of the Prodigal Son, is one of Jesus' most magnificent (read Luke 15:11-32). Here is God's heart completely unveiled. He reaches out to the most unjustifiably rebellious and miserable failure. After reading that story of consummate waste and ruined potential, *now* ask the question: "How does God—Father, Son and Holy Spirit—feel about me, my failures, my needs and my waste of divinely-provided opportunities?" Jesus' teaching gives an unmistakable answer: You're worth everything to Him! Your failures have not removed your possibilities! As Bill Gaither has so aptly said it, "The One who knows me best, loves me most!"

When this perception dominates, a completely different posture toward God can develop in us. When need rises or sin clouds your fellowship, your sense of acceptance remains firm. "Don't let go of your prospect of hope, for you do not have a High Priest untouched with your feelings of weakness. Rather, He understands your temptation, having been tempted as you are. But He remained sinless."[9]

Resolving a Necessary Question

"But," we feel constrained to inquire, "if He remained sinless, how can I come to Him?" That is a wise and needed question. We *should* care about sin's effect on His feelings. But the following verse gives His answer: "Come boldly to the throne of grace . . . and find grace to help in time of need."[10]

"But, Jack," someone schooled in theology might ask, "aren't you taking too light a view of sin? Doesn't it make *any* difference?"

To the contrary, I take a very stern view of sin. The Bible is very pointed on that subject: Sin can never be regarded lightly. To be emphatic and totally scriptural, it was *my* sin and *your* sin that is as responsible for killing Jesus as anyone else's. I am equally responsible with all who shouted for His crucifixion and so are you. Our deeds—your sin and mine—made the sacrifice of Christ's life necessary. So the answer is: Yes. Sin has made a great difference! We *are* dealing with a holy God and yet, all that notwithstanding, He has made it wonderfully clear that we are in His heart and on His mind.

> Jesus completely understands you
>   because of what
>   He went through as a man.
>   Jesus understands completely because He
>   was tempted
>   at every point that you are.

And, hallelujah! This Sinless One says, "Come boldly to my throne and find grace!" This isn't a call to reckless offense on our part. It isn't a brash boldness, but a confident certainty. The word *paresis* here reflects an open-faced, head-upraised ability to come with a full sense of acceptance. And such a posture does not result from a light view of sin. It is the fruit of understanding that *all* Jesus did on the Cross is *so* complete, and its victory is *so* verified by His resurrection, that God calls us to never wallow in guilt, hopelessness or rejection. We are to come directly to His throne!

Nehemiah said then, "I told them of the hand of my God which had been good upon me, and also of the king's words that he had spoken to me."[11] In the same way the Holy Spirit wants to assure you now. God's "good hand"—His pleasure to receive and to work with our need—is upon you.

Standing in Full Confidence

And so it was the people who took heart at Nehemiah's words and said, "'Let us rise up and build,' [and] they set their hands to do this good work."[12]

But just as soon as they did, they were immediately beset by opponents: "But when Sanballat the Horonite, Tobiah the Ammonite official, and Geshem the Arab heard of it, they laughed us to scorn and despised us, and said, 'What is this thing that you are doing? Will you rebel against the king?'"[13]

This mocking confrontation portrays the predictable method of satanic opposition. It is always hurled at you just when hope has begun to rise. As soon as faith comes—"God is *really* going to work something beautiful in my life"—and as soon as you respond with a will to partner with His purpose, you can count on it: Sanballat—the accuser, Satan—will scream, "You have no right to even *think* of that! Are you about to rebel against the king?" This translates to his classic "intimidation-in-the-name-of-Godliness" tactic: "Wait!" he shrills. "Don't you realize your past life has removed your right to future fulfillment? You've rebelled against God's holy standards and now you think you deserve His blessing? You're dreaming!"

But the Holy Spirit will stand by you, just as Nehemiah rose, to declare to Sanballat, "The God of heaven Himself will prosper us; therefore we His servants will arise and build."[14]

That's reason for God's assurance that He will prosper our efforts and restore our lives. *He is for us.* "And if God be for us, who can be against us? Who has the right to condemn us?"[15]

Nehemiah crushes Sanballat's case with the words, "You have no heritage, no right or memorial in Jerusalem"[16] and the adversary's last claim is removed. Let it be so with you. Receive the Comforter's declaration and rejoice in this knowledge: You are now the Lord's.

He is totally committed to your fulfillment.

He has willed the completion of His created purpose in your life. Amen!

Notes
  1. Nehemiah 2:16
  2. Nehemiah 2:17
  3. John 3:16,17
  4. John 1:14,18
  5. See Romans 8:17.
  6. Luke 15:1-2
  7. Luke 15:4-7
  8. Luke 15:8-10
  9. See Hebrews 4:15.
 10. Hebrews 4:16
 11. Nehemiah 2:18
 12. Nehemiah 2:18
 13. Nehemiah 2:19
 14. Nehemiah 2:20
 15. See Romans 8:31-33.
 16. See Nehemiah 2:20.

PART THREE

Sustaining the Citadel

Jerusalem's walls shine in the sun, her glory now restored.
Her radiance a sign to all, her gates shout, "Praise the Lord!"

And I my hallelujahs join; I too am made complete.
And in the Light of lights I'll walk, until in heav'n I meet the One Who saved me.

—J.W.H.

CHAPTER THIRTEEN

People Who Need People

We are bound to each other in love,
By the words of the Father above.
Through the Blood of His Son,
We are merged into one;
We are bound to each other in love.

—*Eli Chavira*

"Then Eliashib the high priest rose up with his brethren the priests and built the Sheep Gate; they consecrated it and hung its doors. They built as far as the Tower of the Hundred, and consecrated it, then as far as the Tower of Hananeel. Next to Eliashib the men of Jericho built. And next to them Zaccur . . . . Also the sons of Hassenaah built the Fish Gate; they laid its beams and hung its doors with its bolts and bars. And next to them Meremoth . . . . Moreover Jehoiada . . . repaired the Old Gate . . . . And next to him was Shallum the son of Hallohesh, leader of half the district of Jerusalem; he and his daughters made repairs. Hanun and the inhabitants of Zanoah repaired the Valley Gate . . . . Malchijah . . . repaired the Refuse Gate; he built it and hung its doors with its bolts and bars. Shallun . . . leader of the district of Mizpah, repaired the Fountain Gate . . . . Moreover the Nethinim who dwelt in Ophel made repairs . . . of the Water Gate . . . . Beyond the Horse Gate the priests made repairs . . . . After them Zadok . . . made repairs in front of his own house. After him Shemaiah the son of Shechaniah, the keeper of the East Gate, made repairs . . . . After him Malchijah, one of the goldsmiths, made repairs as far as the house of the Nethinim and of the merchants, in front of the Miphkad Gate, and as far as the upper room at the corner. And between the upper room at the corner, as far as the Sheep Gate, the goldsmiths and the merchants made repairs."
Nehemiah 3:1-4,6,12-15,26,28-29,31-32

NAME LISTS. Old-fashioned, hard-to-pronounce name lists. They constitute whole chapters of the Bible and make for tough, if not boring, reading. Nehemiah 3 is such a chapter. I was about to skip it, thinking our study purposes could do without it, until I was reminded of a lesson I learned long ago.

I was struggling through the first chapter of Matthew one day—another name list—and began thinking, "What a strange way to begin the New Testament." But I paused to inquire of the Lord, asking Him to teach me the answer to my question. As I prayed, the Holy Spirit helped me to see at least three reasons God puts name lists in His Word:

1. He cares about and remembers *people,* individually and by name
2. He makes promises to *people* and keeps them
3. He accomplishes His purpose in *people* and does it through *people.*

So it isn't a matter of belaboring this chapter in order to wring something clever from it. Its very existence sounds forth *three* truths even before we begin! But there is yet another truth here and it is of enormous value in deepening our understanding of the rebuilding process.

We Really Need Each Other
This chapter describes the organization of the grand, sweeping reconstruction project of the walls. Even though the perimeter was more than two miles around, here is a complete description of how it progressed.

Each specific section of the wall and each of the 10 gate sites were assigned to large family groups or to the members of smaller villages which surrounded Jerusalem. They were formed into teams under Nehemiah's direction, and upon closer inspection, what at first appears to be a tedious recitation of names begins to throb with life and truth.

The facts: 38 different leaders are listed, men from at least eight different vocational callings. Seven villages provided volunteers, seven different rulers lead community groups and numerous family relationships are cited—even a man and his daughters. It is clear that all vocations and a full spectrum of age groups are involved. What do the facts reveal? *The only way the wall was rebuilt was by people allowing other people to help alongside them!*

"Not too original," you might say. And I agree. But an obvious, oft-repeated truth, frequently disregarded because it lacks flair, is usually "oft-repeated" with good reason. It holds a practical wisdom—it works.

The heart of this text holds a call to open up to other people, though it's something most of us fear or resist. As in ancient Jerusalem, we are each surrounded by others in whom God is working His plan. They're around me—and you, too. He calls us both to responsibly, honestly and receptively respond to His purpose in our teamwork. In the process of rebuilding, we will find that our progress *upward* is proportionate to our openness *outward:* Our vertical growth in Christ cannot be dissociated from our horizontal growth with people around us.

I need to remember that I'm not the only person God's rebuilding right now. As in Nehemiah's day, when the whole wall was going up at once, there is a massive recovery project taking place everywhere. The Holy Spirit is not only restoring the whole *you,* He is also seeking to renew the whole Church! The implications of that fact are very real at a personal level, for the bottom line of this text's lesson underscores how very much we all really do need each other.

The principal group with whom you and I are involved is family—our brothers and sisters in Christ—and they parallel the Jerusalem wall-building team. There are those around you experiencing the Holy Spirit's help toward their completeness, maturity and wholeness in the same way He is helping you. And amid this, we all need to learn to interrelate as members of Christ's Body. For some things to get done in you, you have to recognize your brothers and sisters in Jesus. We cannot see our lives completed by ourselves. The Holy Spirit is our primary Helper, but He has willed to use us all as instruments in each other's lives.

I need you to help complete what I'm to become. And you need me and the several others who touch your life. The contacts come through domestic, business, community, educational and spiritual relationships. Not everyone contributes in the same way, and at times, some may seem more a liability than an asset to your building program. But the Word of God reminds us, "For none of us lives to himself, and no one dies to himself."[1] That one verse summarizes a biblical principle which is far more than a mere social commentary recommending mutual goodwill. It is a conclusive statement from the Holy Spirit teaching us that our lives are irrevocably integrated in the affairs of others. If you try to avoid learning what God wants to do through those relationships, you withdraw at your own expense. You'll be poorer for having done so. In short, God is telling us we need to learn to live together. Growth and healing require us to learn interdependency, and we can only gain by learning to do so.

Coming to a Commitment

Do you find it difficult to relate to people, to open up and to break out? Practical problems do hinder some, especially those of us who limit our fellowshipping with our brothers and sisters in Christ as we need to do.

For example, have you felt hesitant to reach out? I often have. And I've been helped in learning to discover causes for my reluctance.

Some of us fear entering relationships or becoming too dependent on them because a past association ended in disappointment and failure. Many have entered a trusting relationship only to be left with the debris of broken trust and with draining wounds to their souls. To overcome the remembered pain of such experiences and to avoid being hindered from our futures, we need to hear the Spirit's call to a new starting point.

The mutual interdependence of Nehemiah's host of workers points to that beginning place—to crowd out fear or reluctance through the "love-light" of God's Word on this subject. Love can cast out fear and truth will set free.[2] The truth about interrelationships, as a part of God's "wholeness program," can loose any tangle of emotions or memories which can obstruct your realizing the you God has intended.

It is necessary that we be freed from fears that hinder our coming to a commitment, for our sustaining a strong life in Christ once the walls are rebuilt greatly depends on our relationships with others. The recovery is only the beginning; the continuance is the objective. We need each other as much beyond the rebuilding project as we do during it.

Submitting to One Another

To shed the light of Scripture on the Bible pathway to relationships, one key subject must be discussed. Because it is so essential, it is not surprising that both flesh and devil conspire to keep it misunderstood. So examine with me the biblical idea of submission. In the last analysis, a right understanding and response to this concept is the God-given springboard to advance and growth in healthy, fulfilling relationships.

To begin, the Bible says that all believers are to "Submit to one another in the fear of God."[3] "Yes, all of you be submissive to one another, and be clothed with humility."[4] These two direct commands teach that (a) your submission is an evidence of your respect for and reverence for God's purpose and (b) we are to do so with a gracious attitude toward other persons in Christ's Body.

Notice that the circle of our call to mutual submission is within the fellowship of faith. The Bible doesn't direct us to randomly submit to anybody. It calls for this spirit of growth and trust within the community of the redeemed; a growth in relationships and healing among those who have been forgiven and who honestly want to grow forward in Christ's purpose for them.

But what does "submit" mean? Is it a call to some mechanical program of depersonalization or to some reduction of my personality? Is it a denial of my own decision-making powers or a placing of my destiny at the mercy or the whim of others?

Those questions rise because for many, the word *submission* has become synonymous with self-abnegation—with a "doormat" mentality. To submit to somebody, they suppose, requires that they grant a license for anyone who wishes to "walk all over me." Any sensible person's reaction to such a proposition automatically closes the subject. Therefore submission is out—the victim of gross misdefinition and misunderstanding. Moreover, human rights and personal freedom are the catchwords of our culture and submission sounds too much like a denial of rights.

But what is *really* meant by the word *submission?*

Although I agree that some exaggerated teaching and exploitive applications of authority have equated submission with an authoritarianism or exploitation, needless to say, this was never God's intent for us or the meaning as it occurs in His Word. Let's take a fresh look in the Bible, for if resistance is due to misunderstanding, understanding may result in responsiveness. And the importance is crucial, for if we reject the key in learning about the real relationship, we may miss God's key to our growth.

The call to "submit to one another" is easier to answer with peaceful confidence when a proper definition is known. Submission is translated from the Greek word *hupotasso* and is derived from the prefixed preposition *hupo* and the verb *tasso*. Technically its etymology renders the meaning, "to place under." But the actual verbal meaning is not that severe. First, submission in its truest sense can only be *given,* it cannot be exacted. A demanded submission, which is surrendered against the full-hearted consent of the one "submitting," is not truly submissive. Forced submission is actually subjugation—the mastery of one party by another. The heart isn't in it. The beginning of a true understanding of submission is in seeing its voluntary nature—a choice to trust and a choice to love.

Further truth exudes from this verb when we trace its historical usage. In the Greek culture, the fundamental idea of *hupotasso* related to fixed positions of authority and sub-ordinancy. It was a basic military term describing the right arrangement of troops for structuring people in strategic relationship; so arranged for the purpose of insuring their mutual protection and their collective arrival at victory.

Years ago I learned something of this meaning of submission and it was through experiencing this very setting.

I was part of a reserve military training program. During my training, I was taught how a small team of soldiers—a squad—were to move forward in enemy territory. Each man had an assigned place in formation following the lead soldier, each was to proceed in a way that so related our positions to each other that we "covered" one another. Each soldier was responsible to perceive his role as designed to maximize the safety and security of the others in his squad, platoon or company.

That military meaning is the essence of the New Testament idea of submission in relationships. It holds nothing of reducing one another, but everything of protecting each other; with being sensitive to one another; with being sensible and serving in our relationships with one another. It includes accountability and is not without mutual acknowledgment of appropriate authority. There are no *doormats*—only brothers and sisters, sons and daughters of the Father.

The Bible speaks a great deal of this kind of life-to-life relationship with one another: "We, being many, are one body in Christ, and individually members of one another."[5]

Being "joined and knit together by what every joint supplies . . . [which] causes growth of the body for the edifying of itself in love."[6] That is *hupotasso!*—the kind of submission we are called to in Christ's Body.

Partnering with the Body of Christ

This was the original New Testament idea in "joining" a church; it was, and can be today, a knitting of lives together in a supportive, healing fellowship. You and I must consider coming to a point at which we acknowledge that the completion of our growth is going to have to involve other brothers and sisters in Christ. In restoring the human personality, I come to terms with the fact that just as Jerusalem's wall would never have been completed without each Jew partnering with the rest, so *I* am only going to be put together through interrelationships with other members of the Body of Christ. As Nehemiah led these ancient Jews in a rebuilding partnership, the Holy Spirit wants to lead us in relationships to one another.

We need to open up to real mutual dependence on one another. That is what healthy congregations are about. That's why the holy dynamic of small-group fellowship is being rediscovered today, for in such settings the love of God flows healing to the members of Christ's Body.

And in that life-flow, there is yet another mighty thing that will occur. Jesus said, "When you love one another, the world is going to believe."[7] He assured us in advance what has been proven again and again. As outsiders see the love shown and the mutual blessing realized by Christians who grow *together,* they say, "I would love to be a part of that kind of thing. These people really care about each other." The net result of wholeness in the Body is evangelism of the lost. Submission is neither an isolated activity of people who surrender personhood, nor an exercise in religious piety. It is dynamic, as was the progress on the building of Jerusalem's walls.

Time and again we read in Nehemiah 3, "After him" . . . "next to him." People were involved together in the repair and rebuilding process, and everyone around could see the fruit of their union.

Today, those who stand with us in Christ are part of God's program for helping us get the job done. We need them, but they need us too. Our submission to one another makes the way for a great building process to be accomplished. If you are not yet in a community of believers, join with a group of brothers and sisters who *are* committed to growing in Christ as a caring group.

Perhaps you are one who has resisted this need for growth in relationships because of having been hurt by people in the Church. Don't avoid this because of past hurts. Unfortunately some *have* been wounded in Church relationships; or maybe just didn't like the way they were treated. Perhaps you or someone you know was even sorely misunderstood or cruelly violated. But it wasn't the "relationship" that didn't work; it was *people* who didn't function in the Spirit of Christ! Those are disappointing experiences, but they shouldn't sour anyone on "the Church."

And moreover, make no mistake: *You* and *I* have sometimes been "those people" who hurt others. We must honestly admit that we can *all* be so blind to our own personal shortcomings that we have probably failed at times to see how we ourselves contributed to some relational disappointments.

There have certainly been times when innocent people suffered great wrong at the hands of Christian institutions— even excommunication without consideration. But the answer to a sad history is not our future isolation. Someone said years ago, "There are no Lone Rangers in the Kingdom of God. Even the Lone Ranger needed Tonto." The need and the scriptural call to healing fellowship is clear.

So, acknowledge your membership. Be part of a church

family and receive the healing and the therapy that comes to the personality through this God-ordained way. Say, "I am a part of this Body" and acknowledge it to the eldership or pastoral leadership in that assembly. Such open declaration is the biblical pattern of submitting to and receiving one another. It's saying, "This place is where I company. I'm not just a religious roustabout. I'm a person who, as in Nehemiah, is next to . . . who is next to . . . who is next to . . . ." And together we will be built up as a spiritual house in Christ.[8]

Notes
1. Romans 14:7
2. See 1 John 4:18 and John 8:32.
3. See Ephesians 5:21.
4. 1 Peter 5:5
5. Romans 12:5
6. Ephesians 4:16
7. See John 17:21.
8. See Ephesians 2:22.

CHAPTER FOURTEEN

Hell's Antihope Program

*Hope is the discovery that everything
God has promised to be
already exists, and all that
remains for me to do is walk
with Him until we come to the place where
each fulfilled promise is waiting.*

—J.W.H.

"But it so happened, when Sanballat heard that we were rebuilding the wall, that he was furious and very indignant, and mocked the Jews. And he spoke before his brethren and the army of Samaria, and said, 'What are these feeble Jews doing? Will they fortify themselves? Will they offer sacrifices? Will they complete it in a day? Will they revive the stones from the heaps of rubbish—stones that are burned?'" Nehemiah 4:1-2

WE HAVE LEARNED that the devil is far more dangerous than the "sly old fox" the Sunday School chorus depicts. Neither is he a red-outfitted masquerade monster, replete with horns, pointed tail and a Neptunelike spear. Far more scripturally, Satan is the sinister embodiment of everything hateful; the sum of all that is heinous and hellish, and the chief spirit manipulating the violence of evil men and the viciousness of deadly disease.

To understand what Satan is like, look at the emaciated body of an African child in a nation ravaged by famine. Or, see bodies blown to pieces by a terrorist bomb.

That's satanic. That's what hell is up to.

Such scenes are not merely man at the mercy of the elements or man victimized by human viciousness. Such strife, suffering and bloodshed are motivated and mobilized by the spirit of hell. Jesus said so: "The thief comes to steal, to kill and to destroy."[1]

Look at a body racked by cancer, shriveled to virtual nonexistence except for slight palpitations of heartbeat. That's hell at work. Look at hearts broken in the wake of splintered homes. That's hell doing its best—at its worst. And when the newscasters report insanely brutal murders or embryos left in garbage sacks, that's hell. But it is *no less* hell at work when you meet people who have lost hope, been reduced to despair or who become so futile about the future they take their lives.

The same "hell" is at work against you, too.

When you study the grotesque signs of man's sin-drunken fall:

- deformed bodies
- ruined minds
- perverted values
- poisoned attitudes

they are *all* the result of the impact of sin on our race. They are what Satan—and sin and death and hell—are all about, and it is your wisdom to recognize that same malevolence would like to crush you—and me.

Every single one of us has been, in one way or another, burned by hellfire. It's left its brand on us all. But Jesus Christ has come to wipe that away—literally, to "Cross it out." By the power of Calvary He forgives and saves, and then He proceeds to rebuild and redirect the potential of our lives and fulfilling of our destinies. While the thief comes to destroy, Jesus says, "I have come that they may have life, and that they may have it more abundantly."[2]

We have discussed how the Holy Spirit brings about Christ's abundant life. Yet many become weary before hell's relentless tactics. Their destiny is in heaven, but they haven't seen "hell" vanquished in its continued assault on their personality. Even though Satan knows his authority over you was broken with Christ's entry into your life, that won't stop his efforts. He will consistently try to hinder God's program for you. Wherever physical, mental, emotional or other personal needs remain, he will seek to remove hopes and weaken your confidence in eventual completeness. This tactic at obstructing the Holy Spirit's work will succeed, unless you recognize his strategy and learn to resist him.[3]

In the person of Sanballat, we see in chapter 4 the satanic style of opposition you can expect after the Holy Spirit begins His work in you. As the enemy of Nehemiah's work with the Jews, his words personify Satan's attempts at thwarting *us*.

Earlier, the building effort having recently begun, Sanballat laughed in open disdain at the Jews, seeking by mockery to discourage them and break their morale. But now the situation intensifies: "He was furious and very indignant . . . . "[4] His mockery continued (for our Adversary will *always* seek to demean) and Sanballat's fury is boiling now. With the processes of time he sees his hold weakening and his capacity for successful resistance disappearing.

How closely this increased hatefulness parallels the Bible prophecies concerning satanic activity in *our* times. Revelation says, "The devil has come down with great fury, knowing he has but a short time."[5] Daniel describes the efforts of hell in the last days as bent on "wearing out" those who serve God.[6] This is not only something we all experience personally, it is increasingly observable everywhere around us.

You need not have lived very long to have perspective on the fact that in just the last few years, a marked intensification of evil is manifest. Youth who have grown up during these recent years may suppose this is the way things have always been. But not so. Even in the reasonably short life span of someone in their forties, it is possible to measure the advancing intensity of the works of darkness. From the post World War II years into and through the '60s and '70s (and as we now move toward the dawn of a new century), an awesome amplifying of sin and Satan's fury is in evidence. So many things, destructive to human hope, are scaling upward as reports tabulate increased crime, violence, suicide, divorce, mental illness, alcoholism, drug addiction and numberless other expressions of human failure. And with each device hell fabricates, another dimension of bondage associated with it comes to the surface. The problem is not merely the agony in each personal or social disaster, but the compounding effect they all have in the damage they leave behind. This can be multiplied well beyond the immediate individual involved.

A suicide scars everyone associated.

A divorce leaves the emotions of an entire family in shambles.

A bankruptcy leaves the shame of embarrassment and guilt.

A disease creates relational and psychological rubble.

All these situations leave remains in the lives of people touched by other's failure, long after the initial pain is past or the principal party gone. These things are happening because of that forewarned word: "Satan has come down with great fury for he knows he has only a short time."[7]

These are the latter days. But I am persuaded that irrespective of how bleak the circumstances may seem or how shadowed the horizons may appear by reason of the Adversary's desperate and despicable tactics, Jesus has bequeathed to us a life of power and of triumph in the resources of His Kingdom. His Holy Spirit is still here to help us realize it! Perspective on the Adversary's tactics is always helpful to avoid being battered and bruised by blindside assaults. The Lord Jesus has not called us to futility but to victory, and we *can* learn the path to His dominion over the devil. We *can* experience full deliverance and joy in believing.

Hallelujah! That's His way for us!!

Relentless Attack

Sanballat's indignant uprising is typical of our Adversary's continuing purpose. Settle your mind on this, saints: Satan never has a "good" day. Some people apparently labor under the illusion that the devil may occasionally relax his attack, as though he might rise on a Wednesday morning and say, "I think I'll go easy on 'em today." But forget it. Such will never be the case. Our Adversary, the thief, comes *only* as Jesus said; to steal and to kill and to destroy. That's his entire program. Wrath, great indignation, mocking—it's the Sanballat syndrome—the picture of the devil.

Then Sanballat rose to speak before his brethren, the army of Samaria. (If you'll alow it, let's simply consider the "army of Samaria" as "demons—the hosts of hell.") As he does, Sanballat makes five statements, each one of which convey a concept which can instruct us in the methods Satan uses to attack and remove hope.

"What are these feeble Jews doing?" His mocking statement is not directed to the Jews, for Sanballat is pep talking his troops. His first observation relates to the tactical vulnerability of "these feeble Jews."

What Sanballat is really doing is lamenting the fact that until now he has had complete control. As long as the Jews had no defenses, he could dominate them at will. While he was the governor of the entire region, and until Nehemiah's authority preempted his, his rule was unchallenged. But now his only point of comfort is that his former subjects are still weakened, though their situation is fast changing.

Lesson: Don't let the devil remind you of *your* weakness when his *real* concern is his loss of power over you! The Spirit of God has come to dwell in you, and "He who is in you is greater than he who is in the world."[8] Silence the snide attack of Satan with your own declaration: "I may be weak in myself, but I don't stand alone." You'll discover as Paul did when he was under satanic attack, "When I am weak, then I am strong." Whatever weakness still remains, Jesus speaks the comforting words, "My grace is sufficient for you. My strength is made perfect in your weakness."[9]

He Attacks Your Frailties

Next, Sanballat asked, "Will they fortify themselves?" Later he will raise question as to Nehemiah's motivation, suggesting the rebuilding of the walls is a latent conspiracy against Artaxerxes. In truth, Sanballat could care less how the king felt. His concern was the loss of his own control and he wanted the people with Nehemiah to think he had the king's interests at heart.

Have you ever noticed how amazingly noble Satan can suddenly become when he wants to intimidate a person? He'll say, "Be careful. Don't you see your *real* reason for trying to rebuild your life? You're just trying to gain independence—you're going to lose real humility. When you get it all together, do you know what's going to happen? You're going to stop trusting God. You would be much better off in need—better for you to remain in a defeated, enfeebled condition."

Some oft-employed devices along this line of hellish reasoning include:

- "God somehow wants you sick because you'll trust Him more when you are unwell."
- "It's the will of God that you have financial difficulty. It keeps you humble and dependent."
- "It's the will of God for your business affairs to be under stress; it develops your character."

Of course, a *relative* truth is present: pressure *does* cultivate faith and growth in character. But the *absolute* truth is more significant. Make no mistake—the devil isn't interested in your weakness for godly reasons. He wants to exploit your weakness, while God wants to bring you to complete strength.

Sanballat's comment, "they'll fortify and rebel," is only reflective of Satan's concern with his lost dominion. It also indicates the incredible lengths to which He will go to create doubt that it is God's will for you to be fully restored.

He Attacks Your Worship of God

Sanballat's third question to his troops accentuates the devil's demeaning, browbeating technique: "Will they offer sacrifices?"

On the subject of sacrifices, Sanballat knows from history that when this people worship their Lord, real power is generated! The implication of Sanballat's taunt is not regarding the location of their place of worship, for we know the Temple was finished and functional. His words focus instead on their walk and their witness. As long as the walls of the city are still in rubble, the liberty of the people at coming and going to worship was always threatened, for it was an unprotected city. Further, their vulnerability to mocking critics was still present: "Some God! Some city!"

Has anyone ever said to you, "And you call yourself a Christian!"? The obvious point of such a remark is that your deficiencies—being short of perfection—should prompt your withdrawal from claiming to be committed to Christ.

And our points of weakness can be terribly embarrassing!

How often have you felt compelled to concede your right to claim Jesus' name—to withdraw from worshiping Him with freedom and confidence? Many of us whom the

Lord is wanting to bring into wholeness, stability and maturity have suffered this sense of shame, and Satan loves to capitalize on that.

This is the satanic spirit in Sanballat's question, "Will they offer sacrifices?" Have you heard Satan say such things to you? "Who do you think you are? Christian? What nerve to openly, declaratively and publicly worship your God when your life still shows signs of the past! You'll *never* qualify as a *real* worshiper!"

But listen, dear friend. Silence that liar with this truth: "My approach to God in public or private will yet be bold, for I have free access to Him through my Lord, Jesus Christ. It is Him I praise and through Him I worship. Be gone, you foul spirit!"

Our answer: "Yes! We *will* worship!"

Slowness of Your Progress

In the fourth challenge, "Will they complete it in a day?" Sanballat insinuated that they would never get it done. It's the same kind of mockery that whispers to you, "You know, you can talk all you want, but you've attempted this before and thought about this for a long time, and it won't happen now, either."

From the text, we are given no idea how long this wall-rebuilding project might have been on the drawing board: probably long before Nehemiah's visit. We do know the Temple had been completed about 70 years earlier, and there is every reason to believe that plans for rebuilding the wall had existed before this. But the vast difference in the past *plans* and the present *pursuit* was Nehemiah!

Yet even with his help the progress is slow, and we will later sense the deep tiredness of people facing a seemingly endless process as they intone wearily, "There is so much rubbish."[10] Your Adversary will seek to work a soul-wearying loss of tenacity in your faith. When things seem to drag on and on, he'll chortle at you, "In a day? Ha!" But don't forget the *whole* story! Times are different now, for your "Nehemiah" has come. If you listen to Him (when you don't see quick progress), and the enemy plays on that problem, the Comforter has the answer: "Do not grow weary while doing good, for in due season you shall reap if you do not lose heart."[11]

His promise is certain. The completion may not be today, but the promise is God's guarantee! Take it, move forward toward tomorrow and don't hesitate in shouting the words in the face of hell: "I will reap victory's harvest because I'm *not* stopping now!"

He Ridicules Your Building Materials

Finally, Sanballat spouted, "Will they revive the stones from the heaps of rubbish—stones that are burned?"[12]

If you recall, when Nehemiah arrived the only materials he brought for the rebuilding program was timber. Thus, and logically, you might ask, "Where will they get the materials for the walls?" The answer is reasonable and thrilling in its significance: the walls will be completed by reclaiming, retooling, restoring and recovering the stones which comprise the rubbled mess!

What a message of hope that picture contains, and its truth applies to you. God is able to so completely redeem and restore, He can glorify Himself in the midst of and out of the pieces of your broken past! He is willing to remove the pain of your past and draw broken pieces back together: "The Spirit of the Lord is upon me . . . to bind up the brokenhearted."[13] The same Holy Spirit is prepared to rebuild your new life and raise it up in splendor. It's true! How often have you heard people testify of the Lord taking the rubble of their failure and building something worthwhile?

I recently made a commitment that not only embarrassed me when I found myself unable to fulfill it, but I was further shamed when recognizing the commitment itself had been made in carnal foolishness and presumption. The situation was more than awkward. I felt I was a discredit to the Lord and to the pastoral office I serve in His Name.

I sought God in prayer repentantly. As I did, I felt directed to simply and forthrightly write a letter to all of the parties involved in the situation—and that involved about 500 men!

Without self-defense I acknowledged my misjudgment. I said I couldn't keep my commitment and I asked their forgiveness. But my most challenging assignment was to confess God's showing me how I had acted vainly and stupidly, and I did. I humbly described my unperceived but now recognized pride.

And an amazing thing happened.

Not only did God forgive me, and the men all understand and receive my confession, but a remarkable turnaround in the whole situation occurred. In an occasion that might have been blighted by my failure, God took it and made it into a building block. Before it was over, the triumph that occurred exceeded everyone's brightest expectations.

Only God can do that. Only God can so graciously yet wondrously reverse circumstances caused by our own failures.

And the present ministry of the Holy Spirit is to give rise to your expectation as well, that in spite of whatever has happened to you, He is able to recover, reclaim, restore, renew and rebuild whatever has been broken. He will bring full restoration to your life, your personality, your character, your mind—to whatever part of you has been crushed, bruised, broken, stained, tarnished or ruined.

He can do that and He will. He will do that even when some of the material is the broken pieces of the life you bring Him. So bring your brokenness, no matter what Satan's Sanballat-like suggestions may be. Learn to recognize the Adversary's tactics. He is intent on destroying your confidence that any of these victories can happen. But through the Word, begin to disarm him as you are now aware of his style.

Whenever he says, "It is never going to get done," don't accept that as a resident thought of your own. It's him—it's the sinister voice of hell.

When you hear, "It's hopeless; too many things have been broken and burned in the past," define the source at once—it's the devil.

When you hear any kind of innuendo, speak Jesus' words: "Get behind Me, Satan!"[14] Issue your command in the name of Jesus. Then begin to praise and glorify the Lord. He is the One who has sent His Spirit to come to rebuild you—and He's going to do it completely. Hallelujah!

Notes
1. See John 10:10.
2. John 10:10
3. See James 4:7 and 1 Peter 5:9.
4. See Nehemiah 4:1.
5. See Revelation 12:12.
6. See Daniel 7:25.
7. See Revelation 12:12.
8. 1 John 4:4
9. See 2 Corinthians 12:7-10.

10. Nehemiah 4:10
11. See Galatians 6:9.
12. Nehemiah 4:2
13. See Luke 4:18.
14. Luke 4:8

CHAPTER FIFTEEN

Discerning and Defeating the Demonic

And though this world with devils filled
May threaten to undo us,
We will not fear for God has willed
His truth to triumph through us.

—Martin Luther

"Now it happened, when Sanballat, Tobiah, the Arabs, the Ammonites, and the Ashdodites heard that the walls of Jerusalem were being restored and the gaps were beginning to be closed, that they became very angry, and all of them conspired together to come and attack Jerusalem and create confusion.

"And our adversaries said, 'They will neither know nor see anything, till we come into their midst and kill them and cause the work to cease.'

"Therefore I positioned men behind the lower parts of the wall, at the openings; and I set the people according to their families, with their swords, their spears, and their bows.

"And I looked, and arose and said to the nobles, to the leaders, and to the rest of the people, 'Do not be afraid of them. Remember the Lord, great and awesome, and fight for your brethren, your sons, your daughters, your wives, and your houses.'

"So it was, from that time on, that half of my servants worked at construction, while the other half held the spears, the shields, the bows, and wore armor; and the leaders were behind all the house of Judah. Those who built on the wall, and those who carried burdens, loaded themselves so that with one hand they worked at construction, and with the other held a weapon. Every one of the builders had his sword girded at his side as he built.

"So neither I, my brethren, my servants, nor the men of the guard who followed me took off our clothes, except that everyone took them off for washing."
Nehemiah 4:7-8,11,13-14,16-18,23

THERE IS NO WAY to completely discuss the issues of personal growth in Christ without coming to the matter of the demonic realm. The nature and activity of demons really should not be a difficult discussion, because the Bible says so much about it. Jesus was very bold and forthright in His dealing with demons, and yet the topic seems to be problematic for some people. Why?

There are three reasons why this is probably so. As to the subject of demons:

1. It sounds superstitious. In a society which sounds the depths of space with radio-telescopes, explores the solar system with probes and experiments with genetic manipulation in its biology labs, discussing "demons" sounds to some like a retreat to the Dark Ages.

But the truth is that "dark ages" do persist today, not as an era of unenlightenment, but as one in which the powers of darkness continue their dark workings. Rather than a retreating of works by demons, our age has experienced their renaissance, and there is a growing willingness even on the part of scientists and educators to admit that "something" personal and beyond man is at work around us. A second dimension—an invisible one—is *there,* and evil lurks within that realm.

2. It seems frightening. As with death, disease and war, sensitive people would rather not talk about the subject of demons. Such temerity isn't a matter of adults being "scared," as with a child at a horror movie. It is more like being startled by the realization, upon being awakened at 2:00 A.M., that someone is moving about the house. The presence of a thief is other than "scary," it is terrifying. So is the demonic as frightening, and no better analogy exists, for "the thief" is Jesus' designation for Satan and his ilk, and such similar subjects as mentioned—death, disease and war—are the stock in trade of this evil host. It would be unnatural if the thought of such realities did not increase our adrenalin flow.

3. *It becomes exaggerated.* It is an unfortunate fact that people make too much or too little of demons. Some mock the notion of their existence; others suspect their presence in a gust of wind or even a sneeze. There are some Christians who mechanically deny their activities, while there are others who salivate with fanatical excitement at the prospect of conversing about them.

The extremes tend to establish positions, as though Satan himself had spun a centrifuge to force opinion away from the center of mankind's life, leaving demons a wide berth to ply their evil wares with the impunity of an invisible criminal. But in the face of this spread of opinion, our challenge is to face the fact of their presence and activity in the light of God's Word and to deal with them in the power of God's Spirit.

The essential need for recognizing the work of the devil through demonic devices is that the defeat of any adversary must begin by identifying him and discerning his methods of operation. Discernment can make the difference between fighting the Enemy or condemning yourself. Multiplied hosts of sincere followers of Christ live a lifetime either wrestling with a character deficiency or experiencing recurrent, systematic setbacks after healthy progression. Blaming every failure on themselves, they fail to see the sinister designs of Satan fashioning devices custom-made to obstruct their progress.

Sickness, financial reversal, mechanical failure, inner depression, lying suggestions to the mind; these are but a few demonic weapons of war. Of course, not all problems are demonically originated. Some natural explanations are likely in many circumstances. And it is unfortunately also true that much of our opposition often does derive from our flesh, as Walt Kelly said through the lips of his immortal comic character Pogo: "We have met the enemy and he is *us!*" But there is more to our struggle than "flesh" and "natural circumstance," and that is why understanding and discernment are needed.

There is a timeless battle being tirelessly engaged in the invisible realm, and the conflict faced during the quest for Jerusalem's reconstruction provides significant insight. Here is a clear picture of Satan's patterns of attack with an answering example of principles for our successful resistance.

Just When Things Are Progressing

Simultaneous with the accomplishment of the walls being rebuilt to half their height, Sanballat and numerous allies were infuriated to the point that they now organized a conspiracy against the builders under Nehemiah's leadership. Their plan was threefold: intimidate, demoralize and defeat. They badger and mock and threaten everything, even death to some and beatings to others, should they attempt to assist the project.

The insidious nature of Satan is present in this pledge to retaliate. There is a complete absence of any justification for Sanballat's hatefulness: only *good* was taking place at Jerusalem; nothing but healthy progress happening among a needy citizenry. But this satanic character cannot tolerate blessing upon people without contesting its continuance.

"We [will] come into their midst and kill them and cause the work to cease."[1]

Nehemiah takes this threat seriously, and the Scriptures record his strategy for defense: (a) he inspires faith, (b) he equips and positions against attack and (c) he presses the work forward.

Again, the narrative's parallel to the practical realities of our personal lives is profoundly impressive. The similarities, both in the dilemmas we face and in the devices the adversary conjures against us, remind us that others have fought these battles before us. And they have won! We share with those throughout history in an ongoing battle:

> Therefore we also, since we are surrounded by so great a cloud of witnesses, let us lay aside every weight, and the sin which so easily ensnares us.[2]

This encouragement springs from a Bible passage recording the names and exploits of others who have fought against evil, progressed against all odds and triumphed by grace through faith. The Word of God discloses a dual truth: (a) all these model the faith-way of victory; (b) they are witnessing our part in the spiritual struggle and are cheering us on—right now!

We need to do that for each other, too.

You and I need to take notice of Nehemiah's call to the people, "Don't be afraid! Remember the Lord!"[3] Then, he places the people in position "according to their families," a tactic combining sound military strategy with morale-building relationships.

And so with us. The Holy Spirit wants to draw us together and teach us to strengthen each other with mutual encouragement. This unity not only comforts, but satanic plots are defused "if two . . . agree" or "where two or three are gathered together"[4] in Jesus' name.

Overcoming *Now!*

Having been exiled to Patmos as a victim of the spiritual battle, John wrote to the early Church, "I am your brother and companion in tribulation."[5] It seemed that the powers of the world—both political and spiritual—had neutralized this warrior. But John's awareness of the nature of the conflict makes him a candidate for overcoming and victory. Not only does his writing in the book of Revelation describe the certainty of our ultimate victory over evil, but the existence of the book itself is a study in present triumph. Apparently confined by an obvious stratagem of hell, John writes of *future* victory *while gaining one* at the same time. His example and message reveal that victory is not only a promise of a future conquest, but amid the present struggle victory-unto-victory is being won right now! Today's pathway is the same as the one in Revelation. Testifying to Christ's triumph over evil throughout and beyond all history, we are shown the way to overcome evil today—"by the blood of the Lamb and by the word of their testimony."[6]

These weapons—the blood and the Word—are precisely comparable to the armor and the swords Nehemiah provided the builders.

> So it was, from that time on, that half of my servants worked at construction, while the other half held the spears, the shields, the bows, and wore armor . . . . Every one of the builders had his sword girded at his side as he built.[7]

Just as Nehemiah did not discount the capacity of Sanballat to succeed in destroying the work and the workers, the New Testament perspective on our Enemy advises serious mindedness: "Be sober, be vigilant; because your adversary the devil walks about like a roaring lion, seeking whom he may devour."[8] There is no reason for us to fear defeat, but neither is there reason for us to doubt there will be battle.

The Bible describes "the armor of God," equipment for spiritual warfare provided by (a) the Cross—"the blood of the Lamb," and applied through (b) the Word of God—"the word of their testimony." Each of these Holy Spirit implements for battle is necessary for both survival and success. The realities of your life and the truth of God's Word recommend complete equipping:

> Finally, my brethren, be strong in the Lord and in the power of His might. Put on the whole armor of God, that you may be able to stand against the wiles of the devil. For we do not wrestle against flesh and blood, but against principalities, against powers, against the rulers of the darkness of this age, against spiritual hosts of wickedness in the heavenly places.

> Therefore take up the whole armor of God, that you may be able to withstand in the evil day, and having done all, to stand. Stand therefore, having girded your waist with truth, having put on the breastplate of righteousness, and having shod your feet with the preparation of the gospel of peace; above all, taking the shield of faith with which you will be able to quench all the fiery darts of the wicked one.

And take the helmet of salvation, and the sword
of the Spirit, which is the word of God; praying
always with all prayer and supplication in the
Spirit, being watchful to this end with all perse-
verance and supplication for all the saints—and
for me, that utterance may be given to me, that I
may open my mouth boldly to make known the
mystery of the gospel, for which I am an ambas-
sador in chains; that in it I may speak boldly, as I
ought to speak.[9]

Stand therefore! The call is clear: *You* put on the armor,
and *you* can defeat demonic assault.

1. Be girded with truth. You cannot battle victoriously
if you barter with the Enemy on his terms. Satan is a liar
and the father of *all lying*. If you become less than truthful,
you not only compromise character, you create problems by
allowing the Enemy in your camp. Don't let him inside the
walls! He's a crafty saboteur, ever bent on destruction even
though his deceptive suggestions suggest temporary gain.
How often have you been tempted to use a lie as an assist?

I pastor in a community where a sizeable number of
people work in the entertainment industry, where perennial
youthfulness often is proposed as essential to personal
acceptance and success. One of my flock, recently hard put
by reason of infrequent work, yielded to the temptation to
lie about age, and even after lying, the actor's agent was no
more successful with casting directors than before.

Time passed.

Still no work.

And with passing time, prospects failed until discouragement and financial distress brought the party to my
office. As we talked, I probed for an answer as to why our

earlier prayers had not been answered. It was in this discussion that the actor confessed to having lied. The force of Psalm 66:18 came to bear anew as my friend was humbled in repentance. The lie seemed small at first but "If I regard iniquity in my heart, the Lord will not hear." We prayed, and this individual made a recommitment to a fresh dependence upon God, without the help of lying.

It's a lesson we must all establish for our walk and our warfare: you can't win against the Liar of liars by lying. Even "white lies" are a lie by definition. All lying is of the darkness and we are called to gird against it.

2. Put righteousness on as a breastplate. The ancient warrior wore a heavy breastplate which protected his chest, blunting both sword and spearpoint thrust at him. The similar rain of fire pours forth in the spiritual battle today, seeking to strike through to the heart with volleys of impurity and distraction, enticing us with evil.

These bursts of unrighteousness are not impersonal objects, but are demon attacks—the "fiery darts of the wicked one."[10] Some are diverted by God's intervention, some by the shield of faith, but however quick your footwork, some fiery darts slide by. And it is then that the breastplate of righteousness is put to the test. The question is: What do you do when evil presses against your heart, when every other defense has failed? The breastplate of "right action"—*simply doing right when you know you should*—is crucial to your victory then.

"Keep your heart with all diligence, for out of it spring the issues of life."[11] God not only offers help for overcoming the Enemy, He is requiring us to join the resistance. He gives the power—you make the choice. So, do it. Let right action protect your heart. Stand against wrong when you know you should.

3. Wear the shoes of peace. We have already given considerable study to what our standing is with God through Christ: "We have peace."[12] In Him we have a warrior's stance of surefootedness, steadfastness and unshakable certainty. Our position of "peace with God" is far more than a "feeling," it is a resource for our fighting to *keep* the peace.

That "footing" is the equipment we are given to advance against and tread down the works of hell. Our position in Christ is not theoretical, it is dynamic. From that stance of confidence we're to move with confidence, move against demonic works and satanic strongholds. Jesus said,

> Behold, I give you the authority to trample on
> serpents and scorpions, and over all the power of
> the enemy, and nothing shall by any means hurt
> you.[13]

The one truly risen and ascended Master in the universe, Jesus the only begotten Son of God, has taken His rightful place, "far above all principality and power and might and dominion, and every name that is named . . . and He put all things under His feet."[14] Now He directs you and me to wear the shoes gained through His victory. He calls us to march forward without fear.

Walk, don't run.

These shoes were made for walkin' . . . right through the fires of hell's worst attacks.

4. Take the shield of faith and the helmet of salvation. God's promises bring shield-like faith to repel the adversary's threats: "Faith comes by hearing, and hearing by the Word of God."[15] That direct statement from Scripture simply condenses to this: If you aren't in the Word, you can't win the war!

Your daily input of God's Word, allowing the Holy Spirit to arm you through it, is critical to your powers of resistance against the conspiracies of darkness. The shield is as strong in your hand as the Word is in your habit. Take it and faith grows strong—and so do your defenses!

So put on the helmet of salvation.

"We will come in," Sanballat's emissaries threatened.

How like those ancient threats are the demonically inspired thoughts, ideas and mental images that often parade themselves before our minds. Unwelcome, unbidden and sometimes seemingly uncontrolled, they seek to induce fear, lust, pride and doubt which can lead to despair and defeat. The helmet of salvation is the armor given us against this attack. How do you put it on?

She stepped into my office, somewhat embarrassed. "Pastor Jack, could I talk with you for a minute?"

As she spoke, I was touched by her honesty as she spilled out a sad story of her past life in a perverted lifestyle. Her present frustration was not so much with temptation to return to that life, as it was her struggle with a wearying barrage of memories and imaginations from that sorry past.

As we talked, I remembered the Scripture,

> For the weapons of our warfare are not carnal but mighty in God for pulling down strongholds, casting down arguments and every high thing that exalts itself against the knowledge of God, bringing every thought into captivity to the obedience of Christ.[16]

I began by explaining that her battle was not against herself. She had felt guilty for even having the thoughts that plagued her, even though she did not welcome them in any way. So from God's Word I taught her, unmasking the real enemy—demons, unclean spirits which were tormenting her mind and lying to her about herself, her past and her present.

Without relating the whole story, when she left my office minutes later she went with a brighter countenance than the distressed, anguished look she had on arrival. The key turned on her learning how to put on her helmet; learning to take the power of the blood of the Cross which purchased our salvation, and applying its provision to shatter the power of demonic "imaginations" stinging the mind.

Listen! When your mind is bombarded, put *your* helmet on!

I have encouraged people, while at prayer, to literally take their hands and put them upon their heads and say: "In the name of Jesus Christ of Nazareth, and by the power of the blood of His Cross, I come against every lying, lustful, prideful and hellish spirit. According to God's Word I resist you, and I command you to go. I am a blood-bought child of God! Jesus Christ is my Lord! You are a defeated foe! And I cast down your working *now,* in Jesus Name!"

Don't dabble with the devil. Demand his retreat: "Resist the devil and he will flee from you."[17]

5. Take the Sword of the Spirit . . . with all prayer. God's Word is not only a resource for faith which defends against the devil, it is a weapon for attack—and *prayer is the means by which this sword is wielded.* Ephesians 6:17-18 says:

And take . . . the sword of the Spirit, which is

the word of God; praying always with all prayer
and supplication in the Spirit.

Two things will help you if you will take the sword of
the Spirit and retaliate; determined that it is not enough just
to stand firm in defense, but ready to launch an offensive!

First, your prayer does not have to be lengthy. This is
no argument against extended devotional or intercessory
prayer. But in the midst of the spiritual struggle, the Holy
Spirit will at times give clear insights for prayer. When He
does, stop there—and use it. Go to prayer at once as a com-
manding officer firing a retaliatory ballistic missile against
an encroaching adversary. Thrust into Satan's domain with
the Spirit's sword.

*Second, understand how that sword is applied to
prayer.* Thrusts with the sword of God's Word are accomplished as the Holy Spirit brings promises or principles
from the Word to mind; ones which apply to your present
struggle. "Praying in the Spirit" involves several modes of
expression, but primary among them is the declaration of
God's eternal Word against the devil. Jesus retaliated
against Satan time and again, saying, "It is written . . . it is
written," and the same method forces the retreat of hell's
powers today.

The combination of God's promises joined to Holy
Spirit-prompted prayer is an invincible resource. The spiritual struggle is real, demons are not imaginary. Satan is at
work, but that is not the whole story, for the final truth is
this: You can stand! You can win! And you can launch a tri-
umphant counterattack!

Prayer is the means by which we invade territory held
by the Adversary and wrench from him the souls, the pos-
sessions, the fields of activity and the tools of destruction he

presently dominates and utilizes. Holy Spirit-inspired and -enabled prayer is the potential of every Spirit-filled believer, but you cannot attack unless you pray.

A Concluding Word

Nehemiah's direction and equipping of the Jerusalemites for resistance and victory displays timeless principles: (a) the Enemy is real, not imaginary; (b) the battle is crucial, defeat or victory is at stake; (c) victory is certain when God's people draw on His resources. The Holy Spirit is your ever-present Comforter; here today to show the way to secure the "city" of your own soul and personal circumstances and bring victory against every satanic onslaught.

Spiritual warfare is no game, but neither is it a realm to fear or attempt to avoid. There is no escaping its reality and there is no running from its implications. People who deny it or philosophize about it are already victims of the battle: They have been taken captive by the deluding spirit of the world.

Paul spoke of the Adversary's tactics saying, "We are not ignorant of his devices," noting that where such ignorance prevails Satan gains a distinct advantage.[18]

One final note before leaving this passage: An almost casual mention is made of the fact that the vigilance of the people was so constant that no one took off their clothes "except . . . for washing."[19] What might pass as a matter of insignificant reference contains an important point of counsel for us all: Never become so consumed with the struggle you neglect attention to your daily, personal cleansing before the Lord.

Preoccupation with warfare to the neglect of fellowship and devotion with Christ can breed an insensitive, forgetful builder. And that creates another kind of problem—one which happened with the people Nehemiah was assisting.

Notes
1. Nehemiah 4:11
2. Hebrews 12:1. Read also Hebrews 11.
3. Nehemiah 4:14, *TLB*
4. Matthew 18:19-20
5. See Revelation 1:9.
6. See Revelation 12:11.
7. Nehemiah 4:16,18
8. 1 Peter 5:8
9. Ephesians 6:10-20
10. Ephesians 6:16
11. Proverbs 4:23
12. Romans 5:1
13. Luke 10:19
14. Ephesians 1:21-22
15. Romans 10:17
16. 2 Corinthians 10:4-5
17. James 4:7. See also 1 Peter 5:9.
18. 2 Corinthians 2:11
19. Nehemiah 4:23

CHAPTER SIXTEEN

Built Up
to
Grow Up

Yes, Lord, yes, To Your will and to Your way.
Yes, Lord, yes, I will trust you and obey.
When Your Spirit speaks to me,
With my whole heart I'll agree,
And my answer will be
Yes, Lord, yes.

—Lynn Keesecker[1]

"And there was a great outcry of the people and their wives against their Jewish brethren.

"For there were those who said, 'We, our sons, and our daughters are many; therefore let us get grain for them, that we may eat and live.'

"There were also some who said, 'We have mortgaged our lands and vineyards and houses, that we might buy grain because of the famine.'

"There were also those who said, 'We have borrowed money for the king's tax on our lands and vineyards.

"'Yet now our flesh is as the flesh of our brethren, our children as their children; and indeed we are forcing our sons and our daughters to be slaves, and some of our daughters are brought into slavery already. It is not in our power to redeem them, for other men have our lands and vineyards.'

"And I became very angry when I heard their outcry and these words." Nehemiah 5:1-6[2]

ONE GRAND FEATURE of God's economy that is much more difficult to receive than redemptive restoration is the acceptance of our own responsibility. It's always nicer to hear about God's grace than about our duty.

Our progress of restoration is measured more and more by our capacity to accept responsibility, for as precious as God's patience and lovingkindness is, He also is set on growing us up. This means we must come to terms with areas of our own failure, where duty and discipline on our part are required. We're not dealing with reconstruction now, we're dealing with life in the rebuilt city.

Any sensitive teacher hesitates pressing the point of requirements, not only because he prefers not sounding legalistic, but also because the human psyche is so guilt-prone anyway. For my part, I want to teach responsibility, but I want to motivate by love rather than by guilt.

Guilt. That old saw, "You are your own worst enemy," rips into all our consciences with such frequent justice, it's small wonder that at times one feels the need to apologize to God for getting up in the morning. How often my own dullness and disobedience has prompted my quoting Dizzy Dean's famous lament, "I shoulda stood in bed!"

Dependent Responsibility

God's call to responsibility is a challenging matter for us to address, because in growing to understand it we must walk a line of delicate balance. On the one hand, God's insistence on our accepting our own responsibility is not a resignation on His part from His will to love, provide, sustain and empower. On the other hand, our acceptance of fuller assignments and duty as we are renewed and are growing in Christ is not a presumption that we have outgrown our place of dependence on Him.

The story in Jerusalem presents a practical case of this balance between dependence and responsibility. The rebuilding program was moving toward completion. Things were looking great! Huge segments of the wall now stood silhouetted against the sky as testimonies to God's faithfulness, Nehemiah's leadership and the people's responsible participation. All that appears remaining to be done was to finish some stonework on the walls, to be followed shortly by the building and hanging of the great gates.

Sanballat and Tobiah were not yet silenced, but they were rendered ineffective; their threats, mockings and conspiratorial designs had all been resisted and overthrown.

But suddenly, an outcry rises. "And there was a great outcry of the people and their wives against their . . . brethren."[3] The ensuing analysis of their complaint discloses one selfish, stupid action after another on the part of the people themselves, revealing behavior that was on the verge of defeating the project from within, after outside enemies had been so successfully resisted.

At the risk of sounding insensitive, impatient and even unloving, let me take two chapters and bluntly confront you with them. In communicating the good news of God's almighty grace and kindness, we are unfaithful to the truth if we fail to acknowledge the point of the gospel. God's desire is to make all of us whole to the point that we are *able* to function in the independence wholeness allows, as ones who choose to walk in the childlikeness that humility requires. This state means being able to get along alone while remaining wise enough to know we need Him—and one another.

Of course such "independence" or "getting along alone" are only relative, because no created being is ever completely self-sufficient. God is our source of breath, of life, of provision, of grace and of all that enables the accomplishing of His highest will. But there is a sweeping difference between our dependency upon Him during the winter of our desperation and recovery from our destructions, and during the summer of our growth into fruitfulness in the sunshine of His life and power. As we come to that season, He will require more of us than before, not because we are independently capable, but because He, our Creator, has now restored us to the capacity for responsible self-rule under His overarching government in our souls.

Disciplined Accountability

Jerusalem was in disarray.

Chapter 5 shows the people in debt, being eaten up by taxes, their children being put into slavery to pay debts, families at one another's throats—and Nehemiah is mad!

I love Nehemiah's capacity for anger. Since he prefigures the Holy Spirit, some would conceivably suppose the prophet to be incapable of plain, assertive, forthright indignation. But this capacity is not inconsistent with the Holy Spirit Himself, for He is not only characterized by the gentleness of a dove, but also as the Spirit of judgment and burning: "For our God is a consuming fire."[4] The Holy Spirit not only can be resisted, grieved and sinned against; He is also quite able to respond: "But they rebelled and grieved His Holy Spirit; so He turned Himself against them as an enemy, and He fought against them."[5]

When I say, "I love Nehemiah's capacity for anger," and note how the Word of God reveals the same trait in the Holy Spirit's dealings, it is important to understand the context prompting that remark. To study the passages cited above, which show the Holy Spirit rising in indignation, we find even then that His anger and action seek the ultimate good of the people involved. His assertive vengeance is never vindictive, but confrontational and bold to judge against evil. He won't stand for it, nor will He allow us to willfully, ignorantly push forward unto our own confusion or failure. Since He cares enough to restore us, He cares enough to confront us. His loving tenderness does not preempt a potent readiness to discipline.

In chapter 13 is a second case of Nehemiah's same aggressive manner as he deals with irresponsibility and disobedience among the people. The first case was just before the gates are hung and the wall dedicated, but, the second is sometime after Nehemiah had completed the project, resumed his post in Persia and had returned for a brief visit to Jerusalem. On both occasions the failures distill to two categories: (a) mismanagement of finances and (b) insensitivity in relationships, both resulting from general disobedience to explicit practical laws of God.

Nehemiah's visit is shocking to the point of being humorous—that is, as long as you weren't the recipient of his correction! Nehemiah describes that upon return he discovers that refuge has been given to the evil Tobiah—and in the Temple itself of all places! Other compromises had been made in his absence, and he moves with bold and deliberate dispatch.

"Eliashib the priest, who had been appointed as custodian of the Temple storerooms and who was also a good friend of Tobiah, had converted a storage room into a beautiful guest room for Tobiah. The room had previously been used for storing the grain offerings, frankincense, bowls, and tithes of grain, new wine, and olive oil . . . .

"I was not in Jerusalem at the time, for I had returned to Babylon in the thirty-second year of the reign of King Artaxerxes (though I later received his permission to go back again to Jerusalem). When I arrived back in Jerusalem and learned of this evil deed of Eliashib—that he had prepared a guest room in the Temple for Tobiah—I was very upset and threw out all of his belongings from the room. Then I demanded that the room be thoroughly cleaned, and I brought back the Temple bowls, the grain offerings, and frankincense.

"I also learned that the Levites had not been given what was due them, so they and the choir singers who were supposed to conduct the worship services had returned to their farms. I immediately confronted the leaders and demanded, 'Why has the Temple been forsaken?' Then I called all the Levites back again and restored them to their proper duties. And once more all the people of Judah began bringing their tithes of grain, new wine, and olive oil to the Temple treasury . . . .

"One day I was on a farm and saw some men treading winepresses on the Sabbath, hauling in sheaves, and loading their donkeys with wine, grapes, figs, and all sorts of produce which they took that day into Jerusalem. So I opposed them publicly. There were also some men from Tyre bringing fish and all sorts of wares and selling them on the Sabbath to the people of Jerusalem.

"Then I asked the leaders of Judah, 'Why are you profaning the Sabbath? Wasn't it enough that your fathers did this sort of thing and brought the present evil days upon us and upon our city? And now you are bringing more wrath upon the people of Israel by permitting the Sabbath to be desecrated in this way.'

"So from then on I commanded that the gates of the city be shut as darkness fell on Friday evenings and not be opened until the Sabbath had ended; and I sent some of my servants to guard the gates so that no merchandise could be brought in on the Sabbath day. The merchants and tradesmen camped outside Jerusalem once or twice, but I spoke sharply to them and said, 'What are you doing out here, camping around the wall? If you do this again, I will arrest you.' And that was the last time they came on the Sabbath . . . .

"About the same time I realized that some of the Jews had married women from Ashdod, Ammon, and Moab, and that many of their children spoke in the language of Ashdod and couldn't speak the language of Judah at all. So I argued with these parents and cursed them and punched a few of them and knocked them around and pulled out their hair; and they vowed before God that they would not let their children intermarry with non-Jews.

"'Wasn't this exactly King Solomon's problem?' I demanded. 'There was no king who could compare with him, and God loved him and made him the king over all Israel; but even so he was led into idolatry by foreign women. Do you think that we will let you get away with this sinful deed?'

"One of the sons of Jehoiada (the son of Eliashib the High Priest) was a son-in-law of Sanballat the Horonite, so I chased him out of the Temple. Remember them, O my God, for they have defiled the priesthood and the promises and vows of the priests and Levites. So I purged out the foreigners, and assigned tasks to the priests and Levites, making certain that each knew his work."[6]

Wow! What more can you say?

Nehemiah was *serious* about the subject of responsibility. He required the people to maintain their lives and their city under divine government. This text clearly teaches how the goal of any restoration program God has is to beget responsible self-government instead of slothful self-indulgence. The Holy Spirit wants the Jerusalem of your life to be a city of the great King—one where His Kingdom life is lived and served.

Numerous details might be analyzed within each of these two chapters, each relating to factors so frequently hindering the growth of sincere believers today:

1. They were financially overextended and victims of economic frustration. Their concern for their children's being fed is commendable, but it was manifesting in strife, discord and interpersonal conflict.[7]

2. This occasioned financial decisions which seemed necessary but which were only creating deeper problems. Their mortgaging property or deferring of tax payments to ease financial pressure was only a stopgap solution that was now coming back to haunt them.[8]

3. Amid the pressures of life, children who were earlier the source of concern now become the objects of slavery, merchandised under pressure in order to meet their debtors' demands.[9]

4. Contrary to the Levitical law, they were demanding exorbitant interest of one another (usury). Their relationship to one another was thereby devalued, and the result was strain among brethren and deepening of debt.

5. Mixed marriages reflected something other than social openness; they showed an indifference to God's order that His people be separate from the world.[10]

6. Entertainment of Tobiah was far different than a social courtesy; it involved an absence of discernment concerning the nature of evil and it issued a welcome to the abiding presence of a decadent influence at the heart of their spiritual experience.[11]

7. Spiritual leadership was uncared for by the people and thereby their effectiveness reduced; a problem that indicated more than insensitive neglect, but was due to disobedience in their financial program of giving.[12]

8. Sabbath violation was rampant, which practice not only disobeyed the law of God, as violation of needed rest always does; life becomes counterproductive, and material interests prevail over spiritual ones.[13]

Determined Fidelity

It is of supreme importance that we understand that Nehemiah's anger was not merely over the acts of disobedience and foolishness. It was primarily over the fact that these same people had made specific commitments *not* to do the things they were now doing.

These were not acts of ignorance. They knew better. Moreover, they had confessed with repentance and regret, having walked in such past disobedience. Chapter 9 elaborates their repentance in the light of God's great mercy and grace, and chapter 10 lists the names of those who led in sealing a covenant of obedience to walk according to God's law.

But now Nehemiah discovers their retreat from that covenant, and he refuses to allow them to violate their commitment to God. His anger is not against them, but is to shock and shake them back to that place where their best interests will be served through fidelity toward the Lord.

Years of pastoring have taught me that the healing and deliverance of human souls is only preservable where responsible obedience is manifest by those receiving the Holy Spirit's rebuilding within them. Nehemiah's anger and action are fully appropriate, and should be taken to reveal God's heart concerning known violation of foundational principles taught in His Word.

Jesus' words to the restored so often include the requirement for responsible follow-through, we are wise to hear His voice.

- Behold, you are made whole: sin no more lest a worse thing come upon you.[14]

- When an unclean spirit goes out of a man, he goes through dry places, seeking rest; and finding none, he says, "I will return to my house from which I came." And when he comes, he finds it swept and put in order. Then he goes and takes with him seven other spirits more wicked than himself, and they enter and dwell there; and the last state of that man is worse than the first.[15]

- Neither do I condemn you; go and sin no more.[16]

These are hard words.

Dedicated Sensitivity

There is nothing so pointed as the issues of discipleship once a person has been reborn by God's grace, recovered by His merciful Spirit and equipped by the resources of His Word. Now, we are nearing the conclusion of this study on the tender mercies of God's Spirit, meeting us in our brokenness and bringing us to wholeness. And I am concerned.

I don't want to conclude in a manner that stultifies an earnest soul with a condemning fear, just as you are beginning to regain confidence and hope. Don't let these words on duty and discipline work against your faith in God's high purpose for your life. Perfection isn't a demand, but it is a goal—and the essence of walking the pathway toward that objective is in keeping a heart open to the Holy Spirit. He will only require obedience of you at those points He has already taught you. But you must keep sensitive to His voice, just as surely as you must walk obediently to His counsel.

Responsibility means "your ability to respond," and where your understanding has been enlightened, your bondage to the past broken and your commitment fully declared, He will expect you to walk as a child of the light.

The way to do so is to know the *heart* of God through His Word. That Word not only commands obedience, but the *heart* of that Word invites you to a pathway of joy and fulfillment that will make obedience both livable and enjoyable.

The key to living the life the Comforter wants us to live is in learning to receive the Word of God with understanding, peace and joy.

Let's see how that can be done—constantly, joyously.

Notes

1. © Copyright 1984 by Manna Music, Inc., 2111 Kenmere Ave., Burbank, CA 91504 International Copyright Secured. All Rights Reserved. Used by permission.
2. Textual material for this chapter also involves the rest of chapter 5 and deals with all of chapters 9, 10 and 13.
3. Nehemiah 5:1
4. Hebrews 12:29
5. Isaiah 63:10
6. Nehemiah 13:4-12,15-21,23-30, *TLB*
7. See Nehemiah 5:1-2.
8. See Nehemiah 5:3-4.
9. See Nehemiah 5:5.
10. See Nehemiah 13:1-3,23-29.
11. See Nehemiah 13:4-8.
12. See Nehemiah 13:9-13.
13. See Nehemiah 13:15-22.
14. See John 5:14.
15. Luke 11:24-26
16. John 8:11

CHAPTER SEVENTEEN

Facing Tomorrow With Joy

*The first word spoken in our universe
was the One which created it.
The same word spoken there,
to this very moment,
holds every atom intact—
every molecule in place.
And that is the word of the New Creation,
which saves,
restores and keeps you unto the
Heavenly Kingdom.*

—J.W.H.

"Now all the people gathered together as one man in the open square that was in front of the Water Gate; and they told Ezra the scribe to bring the Book of the Law of Moses, which the Lord had commanded Israel.

"So Ezra the priest brought the Law before the congregation, of men and women and all who could hear with understanding, on the first day of the seventh month. Then he read from it in the open square that was in front of the Water Gate from morning until midday, before the men and women and those who could understand; and the ears of all the people were attentive to the Book of the Law.

"So Ezra the scribe stood on a platform of wood which they had made for the purpose . . . . And Ezra opened the book in the sight of all the people, for he was standing above all the people; and when he opened it, all the people stood up. And Ezra blessed the Lord, the great God. Then all the people answered, 'Amen, Amen!' while lifting up their hands. And they bowed their heads and worshiped the Lord with their faces to the ground.

" . . . and the Levites, helped the people to understand the Law; and the people stood in their place. So they read distinctly from the book, in the Law of God; and they gave the sense, and helped them to understand the reading.

"And Nehemiah, who was the governor, Ezra the priest and scribe, and the Levites who taught the people said to all the people, 'This day is holy to the Lord your God; do not mourn nor weep.' For all the people wept, when they heard the words of the Law.

"Then he said to them, 'Go your way, eat the fat, drink the sweet, and send portions to those for whom nothing is prepared; for this day is holy to our Lord. Do not sorrow, for the joy of the Lord is your strength.'" Nehemiah 8:1-10

BREATHE DEEPLY. Do it again, please.

Now, touch the most solid object near you, and answer this question: Which is the most substantial and significant—the breath of life or the things around us?

Simple to answer, isn't it?? Life is.

Next question: In the biological realm, where does the breath of life draw its power to sustain?

Answer: From the elements which constitute our atmosphere, as they interact with the breathing organism.

Last question: In the ultimate analysis, where does *all* life find its source and sustaining power?

Answer: From the breath of God which is infused with His Word, which He speaks to create and support, to redeem and sustain.

This quiz is more than academic.

I'm trying to find a way to help deepen sensitivity to the truth that God's voice—*His Word breathed to you*—is the quintessence of your being and your becoming. I'm seeking some means to describe God's Word as *life,* rather than its seeming to be only a book—however wonderful and grand.

To Touch Eternity Today

Please think with me further.

Consider the one thing in this world which you and I can touch that has "eternity" written into its fabric. It's the Word of God. Everytime I take a Bible in hand, I hold eternity, because the life-force inherent in that Word exceeds all time and space: *"Heaven and earth will pass away, but My Word shall not pass away."* [1]

Pause to slowly speak those words above. Pensively allow them to engrave themselves on your soul, for they hold the seeds of the deepest, grandest point of understanding any human being can ever gain. Your life becomes durable, fulfilling and successful in direct proportion to the degree the Word of God becomes alive to your being, life, breath as healing and creative power.

I'm concerned now with the substantial. I'm concerned with the stuff of life.

And the Word of God is *that:* the source of all substance, the source of all life. *"In the beginning God created"*[2]—He did that with His Word. *"In the beginning was the Word"*[3]—Christ was there at creation. These two facts weld into one, helping us understand the eternal truth:

> *All that is and shall be flows to man*
> *by Jesus Christ through the Word of God!*

That's why my consuming concern has prompted my reserving Nehemiah 8 for our final point of study. It is the record of a people *rediscovering* the Word of God, *misunderstanding* it, *responding* exactly backwards and then *being helped* by Nehemiah to a God-intended response to His Law.

I want to do my utmost to ensure that you know *how* to keep on receiving the Word of God. I don't mean how to *read* it, how to *memorize* it or how to *study* it, though all of those practices are very important. My primary concern is that in your use of the Word, its *life,* breath and intent—the very *spirit* of the Word—will fill and fulfill your soul continually. It's the only way to keep the "rebuilt you" built up and expanding.

The Word of God is not simply words, information,

facts and black-print-on-white pages. It is eternal, durable, life-giving, healing, protecting and dynamically invincible. It will last.

And that's why I want to press the point of your knowing how to let it work *in* you, for "Here, in His Word, God has given such great and priceless promises . . . and if their real meaning is at work in you, there is no way you'll ever be less than filled with life and fruitful living."[4]

The Problem with "Receiving"

Preliminary to the dedication of the completed walls, Nehemiah enlisted the help of Ezra the priest to present the Word of God to all the people. A two-day event was scheduled and logistical arrangements made, including preparation of a high platform from which the readers and teachers could more easily be seen by everyone.

Because we're so accustomed to it, we can hardly appreciate our privilege in each having our own Bible. The people of Nehemiah's day did, of course, live so long before the advent of the printing press. Scrolls of the Law were rare, and something of the preciousness of the Word to those ancient people is evident in their praiseful response to Ezra's rising to open the Book.

They worship and give thanks, lifting up their hands in praise, and then they remain standing together for several hours, just to hear God's Word. Whether bowing or lifting hands, whether standing respectfully or listening attentively, the whole scene is one of gratitude and reverence for the Word of God. It was a thrilling day, and adding to it all was the careful explanation given by those who "gave the sense" of what had been clearly read from the Law, helping the people understand the meaning.

Then, what began so joyously suddenly reverses. People began to weep mournfully. Apparently, as they heard the words of the Law of God, they were overwhelmed by feelings of their own violations of the Word and their inadequacy to fulfill it. The situation was one most church leaders would revel in; a repentant, sensitive response to the awareness that God's commands had been neglected. Here was obvious fruit of awakened understanding of passionate concern.

Or was it?

The absolutely amazing thing about this whole incident is that both Nehemiah and Ezra *stop* this demonstration. They speak correctively to the people, insisting that since "this is a holy day," mourning and weeping were inappropriate.

It is mind-boggling! Here is a total reversal of expected religious tradition. And then, as though stopping tears of repentance weren't enough, the two leaders begin to stir the people toward celebration: "Go your way, eat the fat, drink the sweet, and send portions to those for whom nothing is prepared; *for* this day is holy to our Lord."[5]

Incredible! It's like a party in the name of God; one which started that very day and then progressed to a full scale, week-long observance of the ancient Feast of Tabernacles!

This narrative contains a staggering revelation! Leaping from this episode is a mighty statement about God's heart toward the way we receive His Word. The message is implicit. The process of unfolding the Scriptures is intended to issue in our *joy*.

What should we think of this?

We must not overlook the fact that even though a feast of rejoicing was urged by Ezra and Nehemiah, the following chapter, Nehemiah 9, is dedicated entirely to the record of the people's confession of sin, with fasting and manifest repentance. This fact makes clear there was nothing shallow in Nehemiah's summons to celebrate, as though he were promoting a glib response to God's Law.

Yet perhaps there is something of equal clarity we are to see. Could it be that his action, set forth so dramatically, is intended to help us understand something about how God would *prefer* our response to His revelation to be? Is this story a lesson where God's saying, "I want your *first* response to my Word to be one of joyous hope"? I think so.

It appears that in Nehemiah's counsel to this throng, so beset with shame over their awareness of the contradiction between their practice and God's commands, that God would have us learn to rejoice in hope as well as to repent in contrition. Such a proposition makes spiritual sense for at least two reasons:

1. It emphasizes the element of promise inherent in the corrective Word of Truth. In other words, if I recognize my life doesn't measure up to God's Word, and if I choose to obey His will, I can begin by rejoicing. Knowing the "promise power" in the commandments, I can rejoice that the same Word which rebukes me will also release me! The Law which guides me will also fuel my soul with a dynamic for living! There are several texts supporting this truth:

> "Faithful is He who calls you, who also will do it"[6]; a promise that when God gives an assignment to us, His words include enablement.

> "For no word of God is without power."[7] This verse, translated elsewhere "For with God nothing will be impossible," is a mighty statement that contained in every word God speaks is the

power needed to actuate it; the very Word direct-
ing behavior, develops it.

This is why Paul assures the Philippians, "It is
God who works in you both to will and to do for
His good pleasure."[8]

**2. It builds repentance upon the foundation of faith
and decisive commitment, rather than upon guilt and
emotionalism.** This value is revealed in the way the Corinthians were commended for a genuine repentance based
on more than humanistic remorse:

For godly sorrow produces repentance to salvation, not to be regretted; but the sorrow of the
world produces death. For observe this very
thing, that you sorrowed in a godly manner:
What diligence it produced in you, what clearing
of yourselves, what indignation, what fear, what
vehement desire, what zeal, what vindication! In
all things you proved yourselves to be clear in
this matter.[9]

The godly repentance shown in Nehemiah 9 following the
feasting and rejoicing counseled by their leaders, verifies
that a joyous response to God's Word is not adverse to a
repentant spirit, but complementary to it.

In His parable of the sower,[10] Jesus spoke of people
receiving the Word with gladness. The fact that His story
describes these as cases where shallowness of soul brought
no abiding fruit doesn't imply the "gladness" was at fault,
but their "having no depth" was. In other words, depth and
joyousness can go together.

Philip's preaching in Samaria resulted in the entire city

being filled with great joy,[11] and this is not surprising. The gospel is good news, and there is only one logical response to such tidings!

The Comfort of the Comforter

Several years ago, a new understanding began to dawn on my soul. I was seeking the Lord for guidance concerning my own pastoral teaching ministry, and inquiring of Him specifically concerning the mood and manner of our congregation's worship services.

For much of my life, reverence at worship was basically defined as "silence," and the expected sign of God's presence with power was "uncomfortable sinners"—people squirming under conviction.

Of course, I had seen times when His awesome presence inspired me to "Be still, and know that [He is] God,"[12] and I had also seen sinners cringe as the sword of the Spirit pierced their soul. The general opinion seemed to be that God intended these manifestations to be normative.

Although silence usually prevailed, worship also was usually perfunctory. And though souls were born again, there were few saved by reason of having been gripped in a vise of inner conviction. The irregularity of what took place challenged my notion of its being normal worship. I began to ask, "Just what, Lord, *should* be the atmosphere among a people who worship you and where your Word is faithfully preached?"

While at prayer over this matter, I sensed God answering me from His own Word: "Comfort, yes, comfort My people! . . . Speak comfort to Jerusalem, and cry out to her, that her warfare is ended."[13]

The more I thought on this and studied the context of Isaiah's prophecy, I began to see the sunlight of a truth I had never quite perceived before: *God wants people to be happy in His presence!* The continued call throughout the Psalms is to praise and rejoice before the Lord: "In Your presence is fullness of joy, at Your right hand are pleasures forevermore."[14] In the same spirit, Paul insists of the Philippians: "Rejoice in the Lord always: and again I say, Rejoice."[15]

The result of my quest was a slow but definite transformation in my approach to leading our services. It wasn't as though I had been negative or dismal, but I invited and modeled a new brightness. It was not a superficial promotionalism, but an atmosphere birthed by the confidence that when we are happy in His presence, it makes Him happy too!

I soon found people responded with greater faith and commitment, and they steadily moved forward in more definitive growth and service. Not only were our services healthy times of celebration in worship and the Word, but hearts and homes began to flourish in the sunlight of God's love and joy. Somehow, without our realizing it at the time, Ezra and Nehemiah's instruction was being lived out among a people who were beginning to learn the wisdom of receiving the Word of God with joy.

Today, when repentance is needed (and so often it is) we repent; when a new call to holiness is issued, we obey; when the depths of our hearts are plumbed, sensitive response is shown. But the predominant atmosphere is one of sound-minded, balanced joyfulness, and the biblical fruit of that joy is seen everywhere: "For the joy of the Lord is your strength!"[16]

Rejoice in His Word

Joy is the pulse beat to the heart of the message that has resounded since the birth of Christ: "Behold, I bring you good tidings of great joy that shall be unto all people, for unto you this day is born a Saviour, which is Christ the Lord."[17]

The news is *good:*	"I bring you *good* tidings
The joy is *great:*	of *great* joy to all people
The focus is *you:*	for unto *you*
The time is *now:*	*this day* is born a Saviour
And God is *here:*	which is Christ the Lord!"

Dear friend, I want to send you into all your tomorrows with the Word of God in your hand and the joy of the Lord in your heart. *Yes,* His Word is absolute authority and, *yes,* He absolutely calls us to obedience in following Jesus Christ. Nothing is silly here, but joy is appropriate when that same Word is received and that joy becomes strength to your soul. When you have said, "Yes, Lord" to His Word, there is every reason to begin rejoicing at once. We need not wait until perfection is secured, for His welcomed Word will work progressively and mightily in you to accomplish the Father's pleasure. And you can rejoice *now* over that!

Your growth and furtherance in every part of life is dependent upon, extended and sustained by God's Spirit working the sheer power and freeing truth of His Word in you. The Word which created all worlds is the Word which is completing you. So rest in that assurance and rejoice in His Word as He teaches, shapes and corrects. It's His true intent for your response to His Word.

Centuries ago, a band of battered people stood facing the embarrassing evidence of their inability to recover the ruins of their past.

Then a man came.

With marvelous tenderness, abundant supply and patient persistence, He taught them to pray, to resist adversity and attack, and he brought them to the completion of their goal.

Then one day, he led them in the searching out of the full counsel of God's Word. And as they discovered their deficiencies they mourned, until this man rose to declare: "This is a day of God's holy delight: Stop mourning. Rejoice! For the joy of the Lord shall be your strength."

Don't miss seeing Him. He's *there* in that story, and He's here today. He's the Holy Spirit.

He's here as you read these words; here to take you from this moment onward unto the fulfillment of all of the Father's high destiny for you.

Rebirth, redemption, restoration and recovery are only a part of His mission. He wants to bring you to full *realization* as well; the realization of God's purposes, patterns and promises for your life.

You'll find them all in His Word.

And if you'll allow the Holy Spirit to teach you that Word, He'll help you to continually receive God's precious Word with faith, hope, obedience—and with joy.

You can walk into tomorrow rejoicing in the warm delight that God's commitment to His purpose in you is absolutely complete. And you can live every day with confidence, assured of the inevitability of His Word triumphing in you.

Notes
1. See Mark 13:31.
2. Genesis 1:1
3. John 1:1
4. 2 Peter 1:4,8, author paraphrase.
5. Nehemiah 8:10
6. See 1 Thessalonians 5:24.
7. See Luke 1:37.
8. Philippians 2:13
9. 2 Corinthians 7:10,11
10. See Matthew 13:18-23.
11. See Acts 8:8.
12. Psalm 46:10
13. Isaiah 40:1-2
14. Psalm 16:11
15. Philippians 4:4, *KJV*
16. Nehemiah 8:10
17. See Luke 2:10-11.

Appendix A

Map of City and Diagram of Person

This simple map of Jerusalem shows the walls as finished during Nehemiah's time.

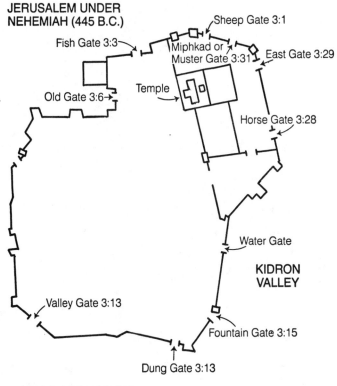

JERUSALEM UNDER
NEHEMIAH (445 B.C.)

Sheep Gate 3:1

Fish Gate 3:3

Miphkad or
Muster Gate 3:31

East Gate 3:29

Old Gate 3:6

Temple

Horse Gate 3:28

Water Gate

KIDRON
VALLEY

Valley Gate 3:13

Fountain Gate 3:15

Dung Gate 3:13

VALLEY OF HINNOM

The diagram below illustrates the parallel between the destroyed walls and the wounded personality (soul).

TEMPLE/SPIRIT
WALLS/SOUL
LAND OF ISRAEL/BODY

1 Thessalonians 5:23

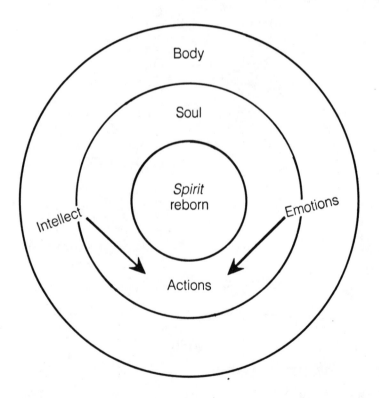

This pairing of diagrams convey the idea of the ravaged walls and the shattered soul.

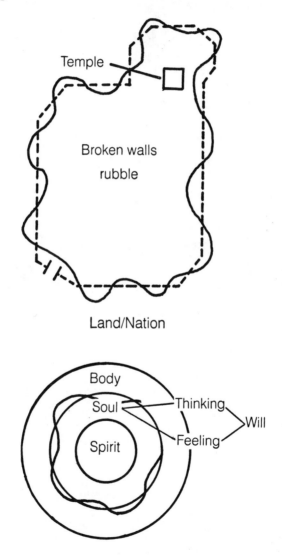

Temple

Broken walls

rubble

Land/Nation

Body

Soul

Thinking

Will

Spirit

Feeling

Appendix B

Where Is Nehemiah in History?

Because the average Bible reader has difficulty envisioning the historic placement of the book of Nehemiah, this is one probable reason for its generally being bypassed in study. Beside the fact it contains several censuses (7:4-73; 11:1-36; 12:1-26), geneologies (12:1-26), uninviting passages with difficult names listed (3:1-32; 12:32-47) or the apparent redundant recitation of history recorded elsewhere (9:5-38), most readers do not know where it fits in history. The adjacent time line and the following brief remarks are intended to help orientate you to the place of Nehemiah in Bible history.

Historical Notes

1. Babylon held world dominance for a very short time (c. 605-539 B.C.), but Nebuchadnezzar, the king who gained that dominance, was the instrument God used to judge Judah (Southern Kingdom) and bring about the destruction of Jerusalem. The fall of Babylon took place under Nebuchadnezzar's grandson, Belshazzar, by an overthrow—an engineering/military tactic of phenomenal proportion—executed in one night according to Daniel's prophecy (Dan. 5). The overthrow was accomplished by Cyrus the Medo-Persian leader.

2. Cyrus (see Isaiah, noted below) released the first contingent of exiles desiring to return to Jerusalem/Judah. He ruled the Persian Empire until Darius (rule: 521-486 B.C.). Then followed Xerxes (rule: 486-465 B.C.) and Artaxerxes (rule: 465-424 B.C.), in whose court we find Nehemiah.

Historical Time Line

Abraham	c. 2000
Isaac	c. 1950
Jacob (to Egypt)	c. 1830
Moses	c. 1520
The Exodus	c. 1440
Entry to Canaan	c. 1400
David	c. 1020
Divided Kingdom	c. 940
Northern Kingdom falls	727 B.C.
Southern Kingdom falls	606-586 B.C.
Babylon falls	539 B.C.
First exiles return (Begin rebuild Temple)	536 B.C.
Complete Temple	516 B.C.
Second exiles return	457 B.C.
Nehemiah to Jerusalem	444 B.C.

Interaction of Some Prophets in the Course of History
Surrounding the Exile and the Return from Captivity

Isaiah (c. 740-680 B.C.). Among Isaiah's prophecies was the incredible advance naming of the monarch God would use to liberate the Jews (see Isa. 45).

Jeremiah (events: 626-587 B.C.). Among Jeremiah's prophecies is the specific statement numbering the years of Israel's captivity (see Jer. 25).

Daniel (c. 618-535 B.C.). Daniel lives through the entire captivity. Reading Jeremiah one day, he begins intercession for release (see Dan. 9-10).

Haggai/Zechariah (events 536-516 B.C.). Haggai also lived through the exile and returned. He and Zechariah stirred the people to rebuild the Temple.

Ezra (events 536-c. 450 B.C.). As a historian, Ezra records the first return of exiles under Zerubbabel (536 B.C.). As a priest he leads the second contingent (457 B.C.) and is later joined by Nehemiah.

Nehemiah (events 444-c. 430 B.C.). Nehemiah is a consultant to Artaxerxes, emperor of the Persian Empire, when as a godly Jewish patriot he asks for release by the king to go assist the condition of the returned exiles. He does so for 12 years.

Appendix C

How Long Was the Project?

The chronology of this book of Nehemiah is complicated and some difference of opinion exists by reason of apparent conflicts in the text. The seeming inconsistencies resolve when simple reasoning is added to one literary practice common to Hebrew literature: the prolepsis. A prolepsis is something written in anticipation of what follows: "The introduction into a narrative of events as taking place before it could have done so, or the treating of a future event as if it had already happened."[1] An example of this is in Nehemiah 3:1, where the walls are described as completed and the doors as having been hung, whereas Nehemiah clearly writes in 6:1 of the doors as not yet being set in place.

A combination of references is helpful in solving the question, "How long was the building project in progress?"

Some have made the sincere mistake of concluding from Nehemiah 6:15 that the total rebuilding of the walls of Jerusalem took place in 52 days. This is an utter impossibility in view of the complete devastation in 2:12-15. It is ludicrous to suppose that a task which could be completed in seven to eight weeks would have been neglected for 90 years.

What Nehemiah 6:15 does testify to is the duration of the time between 6:1 and the completion of the hanging of the doors in all the gates. Chapter 6 opens with mention that the gates were all that remained to be finished, and verse 15 indicates that this process was completed in a little over seven weeks—both a remarkable and reasonable time considering there were 10 great gateways to the city.

We are specifically told by Nehemiah that he served the governorship of the city for a 12 year period (see 5:14), apparently the period of time he requested of Artaxerxes in 2:6. Exactly how much of this time was occupied in the recovery of the walls, until the final placement of the gates, we are never told in a summary statement. But we do know that aside from the delays caused by the resistance of Sanballat and company, the progress was slow enough to cause weariness and discouragement with the massive mounds of rubble (see 4:10). Make no mistake: Nebuchadnezzar's troops had done their job well 140 years before. Jerusalem was ransacked and left as a shame to its people. It was never intended for recovery and looked that way.

It is no discrediting of either God's grace among the Jews or Nehemiah's leadership of the project to suggest that it must have taken at the very least, a number of *years*. Remember, the Temple which they had rebuilt had taken *20* years to build.

The idea of the rebuilding of the walls as a 52-day "miracle" (actually 45 days, removing Sabbaths as work days) is not mandated by the text. The grander miracle is displayed in the fact that notwithstanding so much opposition and such complete destruction, the tenacity of the leadership and the people persisted until the shame of nearly a century of neglect was overcome.

Note
1. *Webster's New World Dictionary, Second College Edition.*

Appendix D

Expositional Approach to This Book

The Bible says, "All Scripture is given by inspiration of God, and is profitable for doctrine, for reproof, for correction, for instruction in righteousness, that the man of God may be complete, thoroughly equipped for every good work" (2 Tim. 3:16-17).

This clearly argues against the opinion of some teachers that historical books of the Bible cannot be sources of establishing truth—i.e., doctrine. The New Testament word "doctrine" *didache,* simply means, "teaching." There are at least three types of teachings most Old Testament historical books contain:

1. Facts concerning the past,

2. Moral and spiritual lessons and

3. Pictures of New Testament truth.

Nehemiah contains all three, and our expositional approach to this book includes an unfolding of a very clear picture of the nature and work of the Holy Spirit assisting the believer in rebuilding life's broken places. This is consistent with the expository style of several New Testament writers and is verified by the clear statements of the Word concerning the content of the Old Testament as it bears on our lives today:

For whatever things were written before were written for our learning, that we through the patience and comfort of the Scriptures might have hope (Rom. 15:4).

Now all these things happened to them as examples, and they were written for our admonition, on whom the ends of the ages have come" (1 Cor. 10:11).

Coverage of the book of Nehemiah has not been exhaustive, since the nature of much of its content does not contribute to anything other than historical information. Nehemiah contains 13 chapters and 406 verses: 189 list names, 38 recite earlier history and 179 involve Nehemiah's action. Thus this study, dealing essentially with Nehemiah, his work, leadership and influence, has only elaborated on less than half the book's actual content. Still, little of the essence of its message is left untouched, whether historical, factual, spiritual or typical.

The following outline shows those portions adapted for the present study and makes it obvious why large segments (mostly census and name lists) are omitted.

Outline of Nehemiah

Chapter	*Content*
1.	Nehemiah receives report (vv. 1-3) and prays for Jerusalem (vv.4-11).
2.	Nehemiah appeals to king (vv. 1-8), travels to Jerusalem (vv. 9-11), surveys destruction (vv. 12-16) and meets the leaders (vv. 17-20).

3. Listing of builders (vv. 1-32).
4. Sanballat's tirade (vv. 1-3); Nehemiah's prayer/response (vv. 4-6) and resisting conspiracy (vv. 7-23).
5. Problems governing the people (vv. 1-19).
6. Sanballat's efforts at distracting Nehemiah (vv. 1-14) and completion of project (vv. 15-19).
7. Establishing city (vv. 1-5) and Zerubbabel's registry (vv. 6-73).
8. Reading of the Law (vv. 1-12) and observing the Feast (vv. 13-18).
9. Confession, repentance (vv. 1-3) and review of history (vv. 4-38).
10. Covenant to obey Law (vv. 1-39).
11. Dwellers in Jerusalem (vv. 1-36).
12. Dwellers in Jerusalem (vv. 1-26) and dedication of the wall (vv. 27-47).
13. Nehemiah returns and reforms (vv. 1-31).

Coverage in This Book

PART   PERIMETERS
ONE   OF POSSIBILITY

1. Rebuilding the
   Real You   Jeremiah 29:11

2. Finding Yourself
   in History   Nehemiah 1:2

Join Stuart and Jill Briscoe
as They Take
The Journey of a Disciple

Christ called all of us to be disciples! In this fascinating video and book series, the Briscoes take a look at what being a disciple of Christ means today. With *The Journey of a Disciple* you will walk in the footsteps of the Apostle Paul and others as the Briscoes teach on location in Bible lands. The questions they pose will make all Christians reconsider how they may not only learn what discipleship means, but live it as well. Learn what it means to: trust the Lord in all areas of your life; persevere in a hostile environment; share the Good News; hear what God really expects from His people.

For group study use either *The Journey of a Disciple* video series or the Regal book or both! The companion Leader's Resource gives clear instructions for leading a group study with the video and/or the book.

**THE JOURNEY OF A DISCIPLE IS AVAILABLE AT
YOUR REGULAR CHRISTIAN BOOKSTORE!
Or call 1-800-235-3415 (outside CA) or 1-800-227-4025 (inside CA)**